Europe Entrapped

———

For
Zygmunt Bauman
Scholar and European Citizen

Europe Entrapped

Claus Offe

polity

First published in 2015 by Polity Press

Polity Press
65 Bridge Street
Cambridge CB2 1UR, UK

Polity Press
350 Main Street
Malden, MA 02148, USA

ISBN-13: 978-0-7456-8751-3

A catalogue record for this book is available from the British Library.

Typeset in 11 on 13 pt Sabon
by Toppan Best-set Premedia Limited
Printed and bound in the United Kingdom by T. J. International Ltd, Padstow, Cornwall

The publisher has used its best endeavors to ensure that the URLs for external websites referred to in this book are correct and active at the time of going to press. However, the publisher has no responsibility for the websites and can make no guarantee that a site will remain live or that the content is or will remain appropriate.

Every effort has been made to trace all copyright holders, but if any have been inadvertently overlooked the publisher will be pleased to include any necessary credits in any subsequent reprint or edition.

For further information on Polity, visit our website:
politybooks.com

Contents

Abbreviations

CEE	Central and Eastern Europe
EC	European Council
ECB	European Central Bank
ECJ	European Court of Justice
EP	European Parliament
EMU	Economic and Monetary Union
ESM	European Stability Mechanism (European Social Model)
FED	Federal Reserve System
GDP	Gross Domestic Product
IMF	International Monetary Fund
MENA	Middle East and North Africa
NATO	North Atlantic Treaty Organization
OMT	Outright Monetary Transactions
PIIGS	Portugal, Italy, Ireland, Greece, Spain
R&D	Research and Development
TEU	Treaty on European Union
TFEU	Treaty on the Functioning of the European Union
UNSC	United Nations Security Council

Preface

The Euro, for the time being, is a continental affair. Its precariousness and the crisis it has triggered have given rise to heated debates across the Euro zone and beyond. Accordingly, this is a "continental" little book that tries to understand the turbulences that the Euro has inflicted on states and societies of the Euro zone and the EU. It addresses the problem of "agency": Are there social and political forces, inspiring ideas, or sufficiently resourceful actors who might liberate Europeans from the trap into which the Euro has led them? The member state with which the author is most familiar is Germany; it is not only for that reason that this country plays a special role in the analysis. The book draws upon and elaborates an article with the same title that I published in the *European Law Journal* in 2013. Among others, my colleague John Thompson has urged me to expand it into the present book-length essay.

Much of the analysis presented here has profited from the works of (and often debates with as well as written comments by) Albena Azmanova, Angelo Bolaffi, Hauke

Preface

Brunkhorst, Alessandro Cavalli, Manuel Castells, Stefan Collignon, Christoph Deutschmann, Hendrik Enderlein, Gerd Grözinger, Ulrike Guérot, Christian Joerges, Jürgen Habermas, Anke Hassel, Otto Kallscheuer, Alexander E. Kentikelenis, Ivan Krastev, Augustín J. Menéndez, Ulrich Preuss, Fritz Scharpf, Wolfgang Streeck, John Thompson, Lutz Wingert, and Jonathan White. Most of the valid ideas presented here are inspired by them; all the mistakes mine. Thanks to Dustin Williams for helpful and thoughtful research assistance.

Introduction

The European Union finds itself at a crossroads between something considerably better or something much worse than the plainly unsustainable *status quo*; in other words, in a continuing crisis. That much is universally understood, both within Europe and beyond. So I am not alone in believing that the current crisis – a crisis that is the cumulative outcome of a *financial market* crisis, a *sovereign debt* crisis, an *economic/employment* crisis and an *institutional* crisis of the EU, its Euro zone and its democratic qualities – is an extremely serious and unprecedented one, frightening due to its complexity and uncertainty. If it cannot soon be resolved (but nobody knows how soon is "soon enough," as nobody can tell for sure "whether we are at the beginning, in the middle or at the end of the series of events")[1] through

---

[1]Thompson 2012, 61; Rachman (2014) reports that while the end of the crisis is celebrated by some on the basis of recent Greek budget and lending data, others, such as an (unnamed) "one of Europe's most influential economic policy makers replied to the question whether the Euro crisis really is over: 'No, it's just moving from the periphery to the core'," meaning that "concerns about Italy and even France should actually be rising."

a major institutional overhaul of the EU, both the political project of European integration and the global economy will suffer badly, to say nothing about the massive social suffering it has caused already in the countries of the European periphery.

There are dozens of academic articles, policy papers, and journalistic essays in which the question is discussed: What is to be done? These often appear with titles such as "Rolling back or expanding European integration?," charting two or more alternative ways out of the crisis, which then are ranked according to their alleged feasibility and desirability.[2] Yet, while this diagnosis of a multifaceted crisis is no longer controversial and "forward" *vs* "backward" spatial analogies are often used to describe strategies, this is less the case with a second observation. The observation is that the crisis has largely paralyzed or silenced the forces and sources of constructive remedial agency, which are capable of *implementing* strategies and changes by which the crisis might eventually be overcome and its repetition precluded. Contrary to what is claimed by Marxian analysts and also self-confident technocrats, the crisis does not *breed* but rather *paralyzes* the very forces that might be capable of overcoming it; it disables agency rather than activating dynamics of learning and the capacity for resilience. The present crisis has deactivated potential crisis managers and agents of change. While hopes (for economic recovery), visions (e.g. of a federated democratic European republic) and calls for nationalist reversals are manifold, the question of who is sufficiently legitimated and otherwise resourceful to formulate and implement a strategy that might move Europe to any desirable and sustainable post-crisis future, and

---

[2] Platzer 2014.

according to what kinds of rules and procedures, is without a widely accepted answer. One could speak (as I have done in an essay written in the 1970s) of a "crisis of crisis management."[3] Even if we were agreed on "what is to be done," the even thornier second question is: "Is there anyone to do it?" It is not helpful to argue for desirable strategic objectives without being able to point to someone willing and able actually to follow it through. As long as we do not have an answer to this latter question, we are not only in a crisis – we are, on top of the crisis, in a *trap*. A trap can be defined as a condition which is itself painful and unbearable to those caught in it but where, at the same time, movement is incapacitated, escape routes blocked, and forces of liberating agency weak and uncertain. The actors have not yet arrived on a stage full of challenges.

What "all of us" are passively affected by cannot be actively shaped and managed by any agency that is endowed with legitimate power. This gap between the horizon of causation and the horizon of control applies with particular force to members of the Euro zone: they are disempowered to manage their national currencies (as there is none anymore) yet unable to establish collectively the governing capacity that would allow them to manage their interdependency in ways that are tolerable for all and capable of curbing the power of the financial sector. Sociologically speaking, the scope of functional integration is much wider than the scope of social integration, or what we are passively *affected by* is beyond our collective capacity to *act upon*. It is the question of agency that the present book tries to answer, if mostly (though not exclusively) in negative terms. There are a number of agents whose actions, as I try to

---

[3] Offe 1976.

3

show, definitely do *not* qualify as plausible answers to that second question. Among them are the ECB, the European Council, the German government, renationalized governments of EU member states, movements mobilized by anti-European campaigns, or the technocrats in the Commission.

The seriousness of the crisis is due to one core contradiction. In a nutshell: what is urgently *needed* to be done, according to whichever of many rival political preferences and strategies, is also extremely unpopular and therefore democratically, within member states as well as the EU, virtually *impossible* to carry out. What must be done, and everyone agrees on it "in principle" (namely *some* kind of sharing and re-allocating both burdens and responsibilities within the EU) cannot be "sold" to the voting public of member states of both the "core" and the "periphery." After all, political parties who would have to do the "selling" are still largely *national* power-seeking organizations and as such guided by the positivistic opportunism of responding to voters' (presumably) "*given*" preferences, while shying away from the challenge of *shaping* preferences, *building* consensus and *forging* border-crossing trust relations in the first place. What would be needed for political parties to shape preferences through persuasion and argument is the capacity to overcome widespread fears, sentiments of distrust, suspicion, a propensity to victim-blaming, and the prevalence of national frames. One of those popular attitudes that parties are typically not capable of coming to terms with is the suspicion that if "we" make sacrifices in favor of "them," "they" will use "our" generosity as an opportunity to take unfair advantage of "us." In short, "they" are portrayed as engaging in the kind of frivolously self-serving behavior that economists call "moral hazard." The cognitive bias of mass constituencies that parties fail to overcome is the understanding that a problem is "their" problem caused by "them," not a problem of "all of us."

The bottleneck variable is thus not money but *consensus* and political support, due to the poverty of the institutional mechanisms of consensus *building*. The incongruence between what "needs" to be done in economic terms and what strategic political actors find politically feasible culminates in a now symptomatically frequently invoked condition of "ungovernability." It applies to *both* sides of the current and deepening European divide of core and periphery. Yet if the Euro zone falls apart as a consequence of the failure to square this circle, the EU is very likely to follow suit. I believe that Chancellor Merkel is right in saying so – although she forgot to add what by now is also evident: It is the untamed and institutionally unembedded dynamics of the EMU and the Euro itself that threatens to disintegrate the European Union.

I

Democratic Capitalism and the European Union

Twenty-five years after the end of state socialism, the history of EU enlargement and integration, coupled with the deepest crisis it has so far faced, have posed the challenge to rethink one classical question of social and political theory: How does the democratic state interact with the capitalist market economy? How has the putative institutional equilibrium of the post-Second-World-War "social" market economy been disrupted and how can it (if at all) be restored at the European level of the EU, i.e., an unprecedented type of supranational political entity?

Following the demise of state socialism, the EU underwent a (still unfinished) process of Eastern Enlargement after which no less than thirteen new member states (all of them, except for one-and-a-half small Mediterranean islands, post-Communist) came under the umbrella of the Treaties and the *acquis* of European law. So far, four of the latter have joined the Euro zone; other post-Communist transformation countries are committed to following suit in the short- to medium-term future. The economic transition they have undergone is an histori-cally novel one, the transition from the "command economy" of *state* socialism to the *market* economy of democratic capitalism. Yet the binary conceptual code of "state" *vs* "market" has helped to obscure the (I would claim) universally valid condition that applies both to the post-Communist transformation and European integra-tion: The market as the mode of operation of a capitalist economy is, on the one hand, the *opposite* of the state and its practices; on the other, markets are themselves *crea-tures* of state policies and continuously recreated by the latter. In Hayek's famous distinction, the "command economy" is based on *táxis*, the discretionary establish-ment and coercive implementation of some man-made positive order. *Kósmos*, in contrast, is conceptualized as a kind of social order, namely the market that emerges from evolutionary forces beyond human design, inten-tion, and even potential understanding.

No doubt, the binary codes of opposing *táxis* to *kósmos*, *state* to *market*, the *"artificial"* to the *"natural,"* *discretionary coercion* to *freedom* has become a hegem-onic intellectual frame since the dominance of neoliberal doctrines in economic and political thought began, on both sides of the North Atlantic, in the late 1970s. Yet the two cases just mentioned – economic transformation after state socialism and EU integration – can serve as perfect empirical illustrations of the fact that markets are themselves *coercively implemented artefacts of polit-ical design and decisions*, not outcomes of some alleged "natural" evolution or simply "normal" conditions. Markets, as well as other institutions of capitalist socie-ties, are *made* and *allowed* to operate by identifiable actors at specific times and locations; at any rate, they are not *"given"* nor do they just *"happen"* naturally. If that premise is accepted, what follows is the need to re-arrange the Hayekian conceptual architecture and to complicate the picture by adding a few items. Let me briefly do so in four points.

First, the difference between the two types of political economy must be rephrased so that the state–socialist type of regime (for Hayek the quintessential case of *táxis*) operates the economy through the means of collectivized property, plan, command, control, and by reference to some notion of "social justice" embodied in *prescriptive* rules[1] establishing *positive* duties. In contrast, capitalist states run their economies through setting the stage for spontaneous self-coordination of rational interest-driven proprietors, i.e., by granting market participants, by merely *prohibiting* rules establishing negative legal duties, the freedom to dispose over their lawfully owned resources according to interests they choose to pursue in competitive interaction with others who do likewise. In opposition to this conceptual foundation of libertarian doctrine, it comes closer to the truth if we understand capitalist market economies as emanating from the victorious political *project* of a ("capitalist") state and social forces supporting it to steer its economy by the organizational device of *private* property, *market freedom*, and the *pursuit of interests*.[2] Market "spontaneity," we might say, is itself instituted, licensed, regulated, and politically set in motion, just as the planning apparatus of some dictatorial party and its coercive disposition over society's resources. The *constitutive role of state authorities for capitalism* becomes

---

[1] The distinction of prescriptive and prohibitive rules is essential for Hayek's thought; he believed (wrongly, I submit) that a market economy is one that exclusively relies on the latter without making any use of the former.
[2] Hirschman 1977.

---

evident if we realize that before even the first market transaction between a buyer and a seller can take place and become a matter of routine, a *state must be in place already* that has institutionalized (at least) three things: *property* rights, *contract* rights with enforcement mechanisms attached, and the *currency* that allows market participants to enter into commercial transactions – none of which can be established by "negative" or prohibitive rules alone.

Generally speaking, virtually every move "free" market participants make in pursuing their interests is licensed, mandated, regulated, promoted, guaranteed, subsidized, protected, legally formalized etc. by political programs and legal provisions, as are the opportunities for such moves provided for by market-related state action, e.g. by trade policies, the provision of infrastructure, zoning laws, schools, research institutions, the courts, and many others.[3] Again, we want to keep in mind that the capitalist market society is a *political* economy, or a state-instituted arrangement of economic interaction. In short, as Polanyi[4] has demonstrated, *kósmos* (in the Hayekian sense of unplanned spontaneous market coordination of the action of interested actors) is not the opposite, but a peculiar sub-case of *táxis* – an arrangement for which some political authority has unleashed the *freedom of owners* in contrast to the discretionary *power of planning authorities*.

My *second* point here is that markets and market competition are, as already Adam Smith knew well, essentially *self-subversive*. As market competition always creates losers and constrains the leeway even of winners to profit, there is an ubiquitous interest of

---

[3] Holmes and Sunstein 1999.
[4] Polanyi 2001 [1944].

---

market participants to limit the intensity and adverse impact of competition through the formation of cartels and monopolies, to deny market access to potential competitors, to resort to modes of "competition" (such as violent rivalry ranging from individual violence to piracy to international war) *other* than the two supposedly only legitimate ones, namely competition through lower *prices* or better *quality* (including novelty) of products. These two solely "civilized" modes of competition can also be bypassed through lobbying for protectionist concessions and other privileges granted by state policies. Also, once finding themselves in competition, market participants may try to acquire (supposedly) "free" goods (provided for free of charge or below cost from state authorities, e.g. infrastructure or outright subsidies) and to externalize costs (e.g. environmental damages, employment risks of workers) without compensating those negatively affected. Market transactions are well known to generate all kinds of negative externalities that are then dumped on (uncompensated) others. In all three of these directions (hindering market access of potential competitors, absorbing productive inputs without bearing the costs, generating negative externalities without compensation) markets do not only depend on pre-existing non-market relations (the legal and monetary preconditions addressed in the previous point) but they also lead rational market participants to generate and profit from *shaping* the structure of markets, extracting "free" resources, and coping with competitive pressures by economizing at the expense of third parties.

All of this is to say that "fair" market competition, even once it is installed, is far from self-enforcing and self-sustaining. If a market is to stay competitive, it needs to be permanently supervised and policed. It is an on-going concern for all levels of public policy to decide and adjudicate on market participants' strategies to evade and obstruct competition, appropriate "free" inputs and externalize social costs – a never-ending task of policing and enforcing competition for which, at the EU level, the Competition Commissioner is responsible. Far from being self-sustaining, markets are utterly fragile arrangements in need of being cultivated and governed by the state's economic policies. These policies tend to be torn between two objectives. On the one hand, and within the confines of a *national* economy and state, they pursue the objective of *facilitating* profitable business for investors because doing so is expected to promote prosperity of the country, create employment, resolve social conflict through positive-sum pay-offs and provide a tax base on which the making of any policy and its implementation depend. On the other hand, policy makers try to *hinder* investors' moves to restrict competition (as such restrictions involve exploitative monopoly rents and interfere with "efficiency"), charge investors for "free" inputs through fees and taxes, and prevent them from generating some kinds of negative externalities; this is the point at which normative theories of "free trade" crossing national borders comes in.[5] It is thus entirely a matter of policy and political compromise to determine who is granted access, what is actually allowed to happen in markets and market competition and what is not. Markets, in short, are staged and shaped by state policies.

A *third* feature of the model of the political economy I am using here consists of the fact that investors and employers, the main actors and initiators of economic activity in capitalist market societies, are constantly

---

[5] Rodrik 2011.

subversive not only to market competition, but also to the political framework of "order,"[6] including welfare state arrangements and policies, which constitute and enforce the running of the market economy. Market agents in general and investors and employers in particular, while being *collectively dependent* on the state as a kind of meta-manager of competition and organizer of smoothly operating markets, still are individually typically *opposed* to state policies "distorting" or "interfering with" the market or "overtaxing" profits and contractual incomes. While markets and their mode of operation are an artefact of public policies, the key agents of corporate capital and neoliberal ideologues are anxious to insulate markets against the "excessive" intrusion of democratic politics. Respective complaints typically focus on two allegedly "counter-productive" and "inefficient" ways in which government intervention is said to distort and disturb the operation of "market forces": *taxation* and *regulation*. To simplify: Far from being perceived and recognized as their "managing committee," the state and both its market-making and market-constraining policies is typically seen with suspicion and often political opposition by capitalist agents whose interests it supposedly represents and manages.

This is where a *fourth* component of my condensed and schematic account of democratic capitalism in the EU comes in. Within the confines of the nation state and its democratic polity, the chances of investors and employers of effectively resisting modes of taxation and regulation that they see as conflicting with their interests are limited. Opportunities for capital to escape political control are much more favorable at the level of a

---

[6] Streeck 2009.

---

market-integrated EU, where its four economic freedoms, a common set of regulatory rules and a common currency apply. Integrated Europe greatly enhances opportunities to exercise economic power through "exit" moves, i.e., the power to confront member-state policy makers with the adverse (e.g. fiscal) consequences of moving investment and employment "elsewhere" in the EU, which makes the use of "voice" power, the power of prevailing through bargaining, voicing demands, promises, threats, warnings, and so on, to a large extent dispensable. From the point of view of major investors (if certainly not all investors, see below) and market-liberal economic policy makers the Europe-wide political economy offers three substantial advantages compared with those provided within the confines of the nation state:

(a) Competitive advantages can be expected from economies of scale, given the increase in market size and the reduction in transaction costs;

(b) While regulation is by no means absent at the EU level (but is codified in tens of thousands of pages of legal text specifying standards of products and rules for the protection of consumers, workers, and the natural environment etc.), the advantage from the point of view of investors is the *unitary* mode of regulation that *uniformly* applies to all agents across all markets in the EU, thus excluding country-specific distortions and protectionist barriers. While the market is not deregulated, regulation is *depoliticized*.

(c) Since the EU is not a democratic polity with an elected and accountable government and parliamentary budget rights, the political sovereignty of member states is significantly reduced, as is the probability that regulations and programs contrary to business interests will be adopted at the supranational level.

(d) With open borders allowing the mobility of capital and labor, goods and services, a rivalry (or *political* competition) among member states is institutionalized, which serves as a constant warning to the government of each of them (as well as national trade unions) to refrain from political demands, moves, and measures (such as tax increases or increases of labor costs and social expenditures) that run the risk of chasing investors out (or encouraging the inflow of "unemployable" or low-skilled migrants).

In short, the enlarged market of the integrated EU provides additional space for action to shape national policy making "from the outside," be it through actual "exit" of investments or be it through the anticipation of virtual exit on the part of policy makers. After *economic* competition *within* nation states has been transposed into the new *political* rivalry unfolding *between* EU member states over how conditions can be made attractive to investors, the capacity of the *"markets" to shape public policy* increases over what it used to be in the confined arena of nation states.

Note, however, that these economic attractions of the market-integrated EU with its elimination of borders and other ("non-tariff") obstacles to trade do not equally benefit *all* kinds of investors and the states, regions, sectors of industry, and employees affected by them. The fact that the *same* regulatory regime applies to all in no way creates a *level* playing field, given the vast differences in economic, institutional, demographic, geographic, and political conditions among the participants in the EU's economic game. As a consequence, some participants are virtually born winners in economic competition and inter-state rivalry, some are destined to lose out (with or without opportunities to adjust available to them), some may be helped by EU funds to catch up, and some may even find themselves in niches that protect them from being exposed to serious competitive challenges from de-nationalized markets. Depending on which of these categories a given worker, region, enterprise, sector of industry, or country belongs, the economic integration of Europe can be experienced as a veritable feast of capitalist liberation, an unmitigated disaster, a problem the solution of which is within reach, or a change of minor impact.

2

The Nature of the Crisis

To begin with, here is a rough sketch of the complexities and major components, functional loops, and contexts within the Euro zone. It all started with a financial market crisis (partly caused by spillover effects from the subprime crisis in the USA and partly home-made within the economies of EU member states and their "wrong" policies), which threatened to disable banks from performing both their function as creditors of debtors in the "real" economy and, crucially, as debtors to their depositors (such as pension funds, municipal governments, etc.). Importantly, the crisis started in the *private* sector – private banks extending credit to private debtors – *not* with states running unsustainable budget deficits and having accumulated excessive debt.

It is in the peculiar nature of financial markets that buyers of assets do not buy what *they* need or desire but what they think *others* (within a globally dispersed multitude of financial investors) will be ready to buy. These others proceed according to the same logic, relying on a mix of information, signals, and guesswork ("speculation") concerning the inclinations of everyone else to invest.[1] The driving force of *beliefs about the beliefs of others* explains the anomaly that, for extended periods of time and up to an often sudden and unanticipated turning point when the "bubble breaks," the demand function for financial assets can be such that an increment in (e.g. stock) prices leads to an *increment* in purchases, not a decline, as is the case with most demand curves in ordinary markets for goods and services. Another peculiarity of the financial market is that the failure of financial institutions (such as that of Lehman Brothers on 9/15, 2008) has a uniquely wide range of collateral damages and social costs affecting all kinds of economic actors who, as the banks' and insurance companies' creditors, have deposited their assets in banks. Financial institutions are first and foremost *debtors*, owing assets to myriads of private and public claimants. Therefore, if big banks go under, many other businesses (including other banks), households, employees, and possibly states will go under, too, as an inescapable consequence. Banks are a structural equivalent of hostage takers: if you want to save the life of the hostage, you had better do what banks request – a plain power relation. In order to prevent the catastrophic consequences of a major bank's bankruptcy for depositors (potentially triggered by their "run" on the bank) and the entire economy, national governments and supranational institutions had no choice but to step in to rescue ("systemic") banks, the business of which many of these same governments had just deregulated and liberalized in the early years of the century, thus enhancing the "hostage-taking capacity" of banks. They were rescued

---

[1] Part of the cognitive input is provided by rating agencies. These operate according to the double-faced logic of sounding a fire alarm and, when doing so, simultaneously fueling the fire.

under terms that, for prudential reasons, were made sufficiently profitable to allow them to recapitalize, i.e., to make them more immune from large-scale crashes and ensuing rescue operations required in the future. Both in the USA[2] and in Europe, banks had been encouraged by neoliberal policies to invest in risky lending (that then failed) by signals of central banks' monetary policy, which had made money exceedingly cheap in countries of the EU periphery in terms of real interest rates.[3] This happened in the economic context of a secular decrease in rates of economic growth within the OECD world as a whole as well as a long-term trend of increasing indebtedness ("financialization") of both private households (which partly compensated through borrowing for declining real wages) and sovereigns (debt-financed expenditures that allowed the economic growth that did materialize to take place).[4] In short, the ingredients of the situation from which the crisis emerged were: (a) cheap money supplied by central banks, (b) reckless risk-taking in lending practices of major banks following the logic of "doing what everyone else does"

---

[2] Posner 2010.

[3] A puzzle that cannot be explored here any further is this. If, as has been claimed, it was *inappropriately cheap money* supplied by a Central Bank that was at the beginning of the extended causal chain of the crisis which led to the banks' reckless lending behavior, the forming of bubbles, their breaking, the banking crisis followed by bail-outs, and finally the recession and fiscal crisis – how can one seriously propose and, in fact, enact (as both the Fed and the ECB have done) *flooding the economy with cheap money* as a promising way out of the crisis? How does it differ from a proposal to use gasoline to put out a fire?

[4] Streeck 2014.

and engaging in "moral hazard" games as they could count on their states obeying the "too big to fail" rule, (c) a secular decline of growth rates in advanced economies and (d) "financialization"[5] as a pervasive trend of not just productive activities in the "real" economy but equally the consumption of private *households* and the *state* relying increasingly on *debt* finance (as opposed to, respectively, finance through *earned income* and revenues from *taxes*).

These trends and contexts coincided with the activation of the third and final stage of the EU's Economic and Monetary Union, the new monetary regime that was inaugurated in the EU in 1999 with all EU member states (except for Denmark and the UK) committed to steering their economies so as to qualify them for the adoption of the common currency, with no less than eighteen of the twenty-six committed to doing so by 2014. Briefly, the arguments *in favor* of adopting a common currency were based upon its expected contribution to economic growth and prosperity. A shared currency, or so it was expected, would make transnational economic activity more predictable and thus promote competition and the division of labor among member states. The single currency would economize on transaction costs. The hands of national central banks which had so far determined the external value of a member state's currency would be tied, forcing member states' governments to rely on adjusting public expenditures and labor costs *internally* in case their inferior competitive performance relative to other member states called for corrective policy responses. In this way, the common currency was recommended for its wholesome capacity to make member states' economies converge in

---

[5] Deutschmann 2011.

terms of productivity and output through inescapable competitive pressure generated by the single currency.

The arguments *against* the common currency, however, and its impact on the member states' economic development are widely accepted today. First, the currency area in which the Euro was established was by far too heterogeneous (in terms of level of economic development, rates of inflation, modes of wage determination, types of welfare states, productivity, institutional structures, economic cultures, geographic proximity to markets, and so on) to allow it to become viable as the common currency. Some countries could cope and even benefit from the others' monetary hands being tied, others could not, falling behind in terms of trade deficits caused by their inferior performance in the all-important dimension of *unit costs of labor*, an indicator that relates the development of real labor costs in a country to the development of labor productivity. In the EU, perfect factor mobility, as required for a currency zone to be "optimal"[6] applies to capital but only nominally also to labor, given the *de facto* mobility barriers erected by the no less than 24 official languages spoken by the 500 million citizens of the EU.[7] The loser countries in the EU's inter-state competitive game were thus deprived of their previously utilized means of running a *national* monetary policy tailored to the specific needs and vulnerabilities of a country. Subsequently they had no promising choice other than to turn to *fiscal* policies of their own, to accumulate sovereign debt in trying to solve their domestic economic and political problems.

However, it was exactly this option of running higher debts that was largely denied to them by the

---

[6] Mundell 1961.
[7] van Parijs 2013.

stability-obsessed monetary regime that accompanied the Euro. "Excessive" levels of sovereign indebtedness are considered unwelcome for a number of reasons. Among them is the (presently unsubstantiated) concern that debt induces inflation. Another concern is that high levels of debt distort the expenditure side of the budget, as much of it must be devoted, with regressive distributional implications[8] as well as severely negative implications for economic growth, to the servicing of debt instead of demand-stabilizing and growth-promoting purposes.[9] Furthermore, it is feared that highly indebted states pose a risk to the banks that hold their debt, making them vulnerable to another financial market crisis. If states are seen by their creditors as being at risk of defaulting on their debt, they'll respond with measures that possibly not only fulfill this perception but threaten other states of the Euro zone by triggering speculative domino chains and contagion effects.

For these and other reasons much of the history of the EU and the Euro zone – from the Maastricht Treaty (entry into force 1993) to the Stability and

---

[8] The *taxing* state *diminishes* the disposable income of the well-to-do through (progressive) taxation, while the *borrowing* state *increases* that income by paying interest on what the well-to-do can afford to lend the state.

[9] Just an illustration: The highly indebted PIIGS countries of the EU periphery are estimated (cf. *FT*, April 20, 2014) to pay the huge amount of 130 bn in interest payments, or close to 10 cent of every Euro of fiscal revenues. This condition makes them extremely vulnerable to future shocks (which they will not be able to absorb through additional debt) and will erode their ability to make investments and maintain social security nets. For instance, the Portuguese state's interest bill in 2014 is almost equivalent to the size of its health system.

Growth Pact (1997) and its various revisions to the intergovernmental *European Fiscal Compact* ("Treaty on Stability, Coordination and Governance", 2013) – could be written as a sequence of ever-renewed yet consistently failed attempts by the EU to impose "fiscal discipline" (limits of budget deficits and total debt relative to GDP) on member states. For, in contrast to the central government in normal federal states, the EU *does not have taxing and spending powers of its own*. It does not even have effective *legal* means (as opposed to conditionalist arms-twisting and intergovernmental agreements entered into under threats) of controlling member states' debt-financed spending; in order to acquire such powers, they would have to be constituted and democratically exercised to gain legitimacy – which is doubtless the case with *national* parliaments and elected governments, who must decide on levels of sovereign debt. All the respective rules made by the EU to limit spending beyond permissible limits (with deficit limits originally fixed at 3 percent and total sovereign debt at 60 percent of GDP) were consistently (and mostly with impunity) violated by the vast majority of member states since the beginning of the EMU.[10] Nor does the monetary regime of the Euro come, as it does in federal states such as the USA, with a policy toolbox that allows for economic policy making (promoting growth and employment) or social policy making

---

[10] Only four countries, among them the two top GDP per capita champions (Luxemburg and Denmark), plus Sweden and Finland, were never in breach of the EU's statutory prescriptions concerning maximum sovereign debt, and the EU-28 average is now assessed at 4.5 percent (instead of 3 percent) in terms of budget deficit and 83 percent (instead of 60 percent) in terms of sovereign debt.

(providing transfers and services). Managing the crisis of the Euro zone without the institutional tools of democratic ("input") legitimation and in the absence of promising tools of economic and social policy is a task that cannot but make the Commission resort to a technocratic style of discretionary rule relying on "conditionalist" levers, the handling of which lacks *both* legitimacy and effectiveness.

The emergency expenditures of public money for the rescue of private banks prevented sovereigns from spending that same amount of revenue on uses that can induce growth and on which growth increasingly depends (infrastructure, education, transportation, communication, R&D) or on social expenditures to bolster demand (public sector employment, pensions and other transfers, expenditures to stimulate the economy and employment), with both of these expenditures at least potentially serving to maintain and increase the future tax base, i.e., the capitalist "real" economy, which to a seemingly ever-increasing extent depends for its growth on all kinds of state-provided "inputs."

Anticipating a further decline in growth rates as a consequence of the manifest shortage of such inputs, some investors have shifted their investments from the real economy to the financial sector (and real estate) because of its comparatively higher yields,[11] causing a further decline in growth and employment and, with it, a *rise* of the ratio of total debt to GDP: As total government spending is *reduced* (i.e., state budgets "consolidated") due to the austerity conditions the EU imposes in exchange for its financial assistance ("solidarity"), the output of deficit countries was *falling* even more steeply, driving the ratio of sovereign debt to GDP *up*

---

[11] Flassbeck 2012: 48.

(due to the "denominator effect" of GDP shrinking *faster* than sovereign debt as a consequence of the austerity measures imposed on member states).[12] This, in turn, has triggered more restrictive responses from banks and "donors." Given the increase of the share of debt service in the total of public expenditure and the corresponding reduction in social spending, it is only seemingly paradoxical that the countries with the highest public debt/GDP ratios are also those with the highest prevalence of (youth) unemployment, poverty, precariousness, income inequality, and deterioration of public services. This correlation does not necessarily have to do with the *level* of indebtedness, as the popular (with neoliberal ideologues, that is) yet controversial work of Reinhart and Rogoff[13] has suggested; it may rather have to do with the circumstances that triggered the indebtedness and how it shapes the *structure* of expenditures, that is, whether the structure of expenditures caters to the interest claims of banks (as a consequence of high indebtedness) or to the needs of citizens and investors. Given the preferential treatment the former can claim for the sake of "stability" (and their readiness to finance government bonds in the future), the debt-financed growth that benefits investors in the "real" economy and citizens is bound to remain anemic and largely "jobless."[14]

The monetary regime of the Euro can thus be described (and as of early 2014 largely uncontroversially so) as suffering from *two major defects*: it is built in the "wrong," at least *by far sub-optimal currency area* of a highly inhomogeneous economic

---

[12] Blanchard and Leigh 2013.
[13] Reinhart and Rogoff 2010.
[14] International Labour Organization 2014.

space[15] the divergence of which it further propels; and it is *institutionally* deficient as its *policy making capacity is severely limited* in the areas of fiscal, economic, and social policies. Not only does the Euro tie the hands of national central banks to perform monetary policies of their own tailored to their needs; it also ties the hands of European policy makers to compensate for the damages the Euro inflicts upon the losers of the new monetary game. Only rabid market ideologues believe in the "automatic" adjustment of socioeconomic imbalances across regions and countries in Europe, be it through the lowering of wages and prices in the less prosperous parts of the system or through outward migration of labor to the more prosperous ones. Policy capacities are needed to make persistent imbalances bearable. These policy competencies (in the absence of which the playing field of the Euro game is allowed to become ever more tilted against the deficit countries) would also be required to promote convergence in more vigorous ways than can possibly be accomplished with the seriously inadequate means available through the EU's Structural Funds and Cohesion Fund. But such acquisition of new competencies is inconceivable without them being executed in ways that are democratically accountable to European citizens and member states.

As to the first defect, the Euro under the ECB's regime over-generalizes monetary policy across widely

---

[15] To use just one indicator for illustration: GDP per capita relates from the (admittedly: outlier of) Luxemburg at the peak to Bulgaria at the bottom as 17 relates to 1, with 10 of the 12 new member states together making up the lower end of the distribution, indicating the persistent East–West divide within the EU.

---

diverging economies and their given position in the business cycle. Instead of the "one size fits all" we are left with a situation where "one size fits *none*" due to the institutional incapacity of monetary policy to respond to the *specifics* of countries and their situations.[16] The regime lacks institutional tools that would allow it to apply differentiated measures at specific points in time and space so as to absorb "asymmetric shocks" and "bubbles," as well as the capacity to address country-specific rates of inflation or fiscal expansion. In fact, far from being just an apolitical device of easy and reliable payment among private and public entities across a large territorial domain, the Euro, *dis*uniting as it is its zone by its common currency, is itself in need of justification in view of its substantial distributive, more precisely: *regressively* redistributive effects. It divides Euro-Europe into the "core" or "surplus" countries of Germany, Austria, Finland, the Netherlands, and Luxemburg and pits them against the "periphery" or "deficit" member states in the southern and western (Ireland) "peripheries." It privileges the former by affording them to profit from a single external exchange rate, which, in the absence of the Euro and after their hypothetical return to national currencies, would be far less favorable in their goal of achieving export surpluses, in which they currently excel under the Euro regime. At the same time, the Euro system forecloses the option of periphery countries ever to exit the Euro zone (other than by a state declaring its insolvency, thereby losing all its creditability with the very banks on whom they so desperately depend). As the deficit countries are virtually trapped in the single currency, it provides cheap credit to core economies and their states at single interest rates for ECB money, the setting of which

---

[16] Scharpf 2011; Enderlein 2013a.

at close-to-zero percent have been primarily motivated by the need to stimulate growth in the periphery. While the desired effect of providing cheap money has not materialized there due to lenders' lack of confidence in the prospects of a sustained recovery of the south, the winners of this monetary policy are economies and states to the north of the new European divide. For instance, the Netherlands have reportedly saved 7.5 billion Euros in interest payments from 2007 to 2011; in Germany this amount is estimated at 15 to 20 billion Euros.[17] Moreover, private financial investors will privilege states for investment that they consider reliably able to sustain and service debt over those they consider less fortunate. For all these reasons and built-in discriminatory biases, the very institutional arrangement of the Euro is bound to generate growing volumes of conflict for which, however, it denies (constrained as it is by the legalistic veto power of national constitutional courts and the intergovernmental unanimity rule governing the European Council) any kind of institutionalized political outlet.

As to the second defect, lacking the democratic legitimacy that would be needed for the making of economic and social policies, the EU cannot even legally coerce member state governments to adhere to the debt rules which these governments often positively *need* to violate in order to prevent the social and economic disasters that would result (and have massively resulted already) from greater compliance with austerity rules. The problem is not that political elites are opportunistic and profligate over-spenders. The problem is that the institutional machinery of democratic capitalism, given the dependency of capital upon the state highlighted above, evidently depends ever more on sovereign debt as its fuel.

---

[17] Mak 2012: 15.

Capitalist democracies with open borders are essentially addicted to ever-deeper sovereign indebtedness. This is so for both "democratic" and "capitalist" reasons, as James O'Connor[18] has argued more than a generation ago. As to the former of these reasons, there are clear political limits to cuts of transfers and social protection, burdens of indirect taxation, and welfare state retrenchment moves that national governments are ready and able to impose on their populations; after all, governments and the political parties on which they are based strive to be re-elected. As to the latter, investment, accumulation, employment, and ultimately the future tax base of states all critically depend on public expenditures for all kinds of infrastructure investment in the broadest sense; at the same time, the financial option of taxing wealth and corporate capital as an alternative to debt financing is largely precluded (in all but a few fortunate yet exceptional Scandinavian cases) by the capital mobility and options of tax evasion that fiscal policy makers must keep in mind and respect. The contradiction is this: In order to obtain credit by issuing government bonds, sovereigns must commit themselves to spending growing portions of tax revenues (which would otherwise be available for boosting both demand and supply in the real economy) on servicing their debt. Also, they become dependent on the creditors' assessment of the "health" of their economy, financial investors' perceptions concerning the conduciveness of government policies to economic growth and hence the growth of the tax base needed to pay interest and eventually pay back their debts. Yet nobody seems to have a clear idea about how such growth can be brought about, be it (in particular) at the regional, at the member

---

[18] O'Connor 1979.

state or the EU level – least of all under a regime of austerity that is devoid of adequate elements of redistributive fiscal federalism.

The conditionalist strategy of the "Troika" toward the peripheral countries of the Euro zone has consisted of two demands that must be satisfied as a *quid pro quo* of debt relief and financial assistance: austerity and "structural reform." It is common knowledge by now that austerity has plain negative effects upon growth and employment. As to "reform," there is new and already ubiquitous semantics. It used to be the case that by the term "reform" we meant something proactive and "progressive," even a step toward greater distributional justice. Now we see that the opposite is meant by reform: cutting down on welfare and the deregulation of markets for goods, services, and, in particular, labor. That is to say: "Making it easier to fire labor or start new businesses, liberalization of closed professions, and removal of controls on markets for goods and services." Although such "reforms" may contribute to long-term gains in productivity and competitiveness, their short-term effect is, as Rodrik has argued,[19] the shedding of labor which cannot be absorbed by alternative employers as long as the latter "have difficulty finding consumers" – in addition to, one might add, the related difficulty of finding affordable credit needed for setting up "new businesses."

Yet virtually the entire political elite of Europe and of member states continues to proclaim that reforms (in the new sense) are necessary, urgently called for, and unavoidable. To be sure, there cannot be any reasonable doubt that a modern capitalist economy depends for its viability on a Weberian "rational" type

---

[19] Rodrik 2013.

---

of administration and the enforcement of rules that apply to all. In contrast, nepotism, corruption, the sale of offices and court decisions, the effective resistance of privileged social actors against the tax law or criminal laws to be enforced against them, clientelistic protection of privileges, and other particularist practices are costly in their economic consequences and, uncontroversially, deserve to be eradicated where they have survived. In order to meet this challenge of modernization, however, the *state* and its rule-making and rule enforcement capacity need to be strengthened, not *market* forces unleashed. What is to be protected is the security of the least privileged, not the status of those resourceful enough to "buy" protection and privilege. This essential difference tends to be neglected in the new conditionalist reformism of the EU, which exposes to "markets", in the name of "internal devaluation," exactly those (youth, pensioners, the clients of public services, laid-off public sector workers, and so on) who are most vulnerable and least equipped to cope. Besides, whatever the economic virtues of any reform proposal may be held to be, such proposals are most unlikely to be adopted and readily complied with if they are promoted not by a democratic political process of legislation but by foreign imposition and perceived blackmail, to which the reaction has often been a sense of intense humiliation, indignation, and anger. Also, "in a shrinking economy structural reform is very difficult to carry through...In times of rapidly rising unemployment and cuts in welfare expenditure, reform is more likely to make things worse."[20] Who deserves to be protected from market forces and who doesn't (and who is to be empowered to cope with them through, for instance,

---

[20] Tsoukalis 2014: 45f.

The Nature of the Crisis

education and training services or access to affordable credit) is a question of political debate and struggle at the national and EU levels, one that can neither legitimately nor effectively be answered by technocrats in the Commission and their prescriptions for "reform."

Apart from the regressive distributional effects, unmet needs, and often the outright misery that is being inflicted by "reforms" on the recipients of wages, pensions, and services, their alleged beneficial effect upon the economies of Europe's peripheral countries is far from obvious. True, reforms can increase labor productivity, as measured by total labor cost per unit of output. For instance, if job protection is abolished, employers save wages for labor they do not need any longer due to a decline in demand. To them, adjustment to contracting markets becomes less expensive than it would be in the absence of "reform." But unless there is sufficient effective demand, domestic or foreign, to pick up the (presumably) cheaper output of more productive workers – which is a big "if" – the net effect of reform is less employment, rather than economic recovery through enhanced productivity, leading to greater competitiveness and eventually additional employment. Or employers would have to use gains from enhanced productivity for granting proportionally higher wages to their now more productive work force (unlikely under conditions of high unemployment) or use them for additional job-creating investment, which they are unlikely to do unless they anticipate additional demand. The wide-open question is whether effective demand, as it is *depressed* by productivity-enhancing labor market reforms, will be adequately compensated for by greater competitive success in the marketing of goods and services. In the absence of favorable anticipations to that effect, "reforms" (like fiscal austerity measures) will just depress demand further.

3
Growth, Debt, and Doom Loops

There is a complex tangle of doom loops unfolding among the four macro types of economic agents. These are (a) the financial industries, (b) the state and its fiscal authorities, (c) the "real" economy, consisting of investors, workers, and consumers and (d) the citizenry of national representative democracies.

Private investors and consumers vs creditors: "Financialization" has become a widely used descriptor of dominant trends in advanced capitalist economies. In one of the several meanings of the term, it refers to the volume of aggregate liabilities relative to GDP. This volume – the total of debt incurred by households, investors, states, and banks – has roughly doubled in the course of the last four decades in economies of the USA or Germany: from the factor of 4.5 to the zfactor of 9.[1] That is to say: total debt, equal to the total assets of banks, amounts to about nine times the annual GDP.

The private sector (made up of producers and workers/consumers) depends on credit, taken out by manufacturing and commercial enterprises for physical investment and commerce and by private households for

---

[1] Streeck 2014.

consumption. Private production and consumption is increasingly based on credit, which is nothing but (*expected*) future income that is presently spent under the promise to pay it back with interest out of (*realized*) future income. Households and investors depend on creditors. Inversely, the readiness of banks actually to grant credit depends on lenders being provided with a – credi(ta)ble – "business plan" or (in the case of private households) employment prospects that assure creditors of the future ability of borrowers to service and eventually pay back their debt: financial institutions depend on the viability of business plans/ employment prospects of debtors. To the extent banks see reasons to doubt the creditability of borrowers, they will increase interest rates or ask for collaterals that reflect their assessment of risk. Yet, facing the burden of high interest rates, investors in the "real" economy will find it ever harder to provide a business plan that satisfies banks. The resulting credit crunch deepens the recession in ways that cannot be compensated for by even negative real interest rates offered to the banks by the ECB. If satisfactory (micro) profitability or (macro) prospects for GDP growth are seen by banks as dubious, there is no reason for them to grant credit to private-sector actors.[2] In anticipation of ECB stress tests being administered to them and mindful of all the loans that performed badly in the past, many banks try to improve their capital buffer and thus become all the more risk-averse. They turn to investing in government debt instead of financing

---

[2] Sarah Gordon (2014) quotes a senior banking expert as saying: "Credit growth isn't going to lead the recovery. The recovery has to happen first." Yet as the recovery itself depends on affordable credit, it has questionable chance to "happen first."

SMEs. A preference for investing in sovereign debt may also be suggested by the fact that, given crisis-ridden sovereigns' ongoing demand for credit, lenders anticipate comparatively greater profits from crediting sovereigns than from crediting investors in the "real" economy.

Growth, employment, and the competitiveness of national economies, however, have come to depend, in "mature" capitalist economies, not just on bank-provided credit but (increasingly) also on state-financed infrastructure investments in a wide sense (comprising investment for transportation and communication, cheap energy, research and development, education, and skill formation, defense spending). Today, the question is wide open, given climate and resource constraints and dynamics of global competition, whether rates of economic growth that are sufficient to satisfy lenders' expectations can at all be achieved in OECD economies through "growth programs" involving all those state-provided inputs. Equally open is the question of whether growth rates sufficient for (or a tolerable approximation to) "full" employment can be achieved; however, if this were the case, will banks find it profitable to step up effective demand through granting consumer credit to private households?

Moreover, to the extent that growth rates are at all positive on long-term average, their sources tend to be increasingly regionally concentrated within and among countries. This trend of growth being increasingly concentrated in space also seems to apply at the global level: Almost half of global GDP growth has originated in 2011 from just two of the BRIC countries alone, India and China[3] – more precisely: disproportionately from relatively small productive core regions within these countries. Within the EU, the substantial resources allocated by the

---

[3] Giles and Allen 2013.

EU's structural funds to countries, regions within countries, industries and infrastructure projects have not contributed to convergence, even failed to halt the ongoing divergence between core and peripheries in terms of competitiveness and growth performance. Calls for a "Marshall plan for Greece" (or southern Italy or any other peripheral region within the EU or its member states) fail to fall on credi(ta)ble soil because the question is exceedingly hard to answer concerning what sector of industry, exactly, it is that is expected to flourish in, say, the Peloponnese, Calabria or, for that matter, the north-eastern German *Land* of Mecklenburg-Vorpommern. If economic growth becomes regionally concentrated and insular, both on a global scale[4] and within countries, expensive state-sponsored programs (such as agricultural subsidies) are called for, which are designed to somewhat equalize conditions in the spatial dimension – among other reasons, in order to discourage excessive internal migration. Similarly, in order to maintain levels of demand that can sustain growth, minimally redistributive tax and social policies are needed (yet hard to finance) in societies characterized by growing unemployment, income inequality, poverty, precariousness, and demographic imbalances.

A plausible scenario is that the OECD world is moving toward the kind of society in which growing numbers of poor people (together with a credit-card-owning consumerist middle class) rely, to the extent they can afford it, on credit, and, decreasingly, transfers, in order to cover consumption needs; a tiny category of peak earners (the proverbial "one percent" in the USA), who have

---

[4] By 2017, it is predicted that "the world's top 10 countries by share of global growth will have shifted entirely out of Europe and the whole EU is expected to account for only 5.7 per cent of world growth." (Giles and Allen, 2013.)

no conceivable use for their (at best moderately taxed) income other than financial investments; and a few young *"entrepreneurs"*, who manage to take out credit to invest in the real economy, while being increasingly outnumbered by elderly *"rentiers"*, who are primarily interested in a steady flow of safe income from financial investments rather than "profits"[5] from activities in the "real" economy. It has been argued by Deutschmann that the shift of the financial industry from financing investments in the "real" economy to financing sovereign debt and speculative trading in debt is due to a relative shortage of "classical" debtors – debtors who take out loans in order to finance investment in productive activities, the returns from which allow them to service their debt. This shortage of demand for credit in the "real" economy can arguably be attributed to the combined effect of the demographic change of aging societies (wealthy pensioners are much more inclined to act as *rentiers* rather than as entrepreneurs), plus a secular decline of economic growth rates throughout the OECD world (as Robert J. Gordon[6] has argued in an influential paper on US long-term growth prospects). To deepen the dilemma even further, let me just point to the currently widely shared doubts about whether we in the advanced societies can *afford* growth ("as we know it") at all, for environmental and, in particular, climate-change considerations. Taking these considerations together, we get three propositions, each of which is as plausible as they are mutually incompatible: (1) growth is indispensable, (2) growth rates are approximating zero in advanced economies, (3) growth becomes unaffordable in view of its negative externalities.

---

[5] Deutschmann 2011.
[6] Gordon 2012.

Creditors vs sovereign states: After failed investments and burst bubbles suffered by the financial industry, the state needs to rescue/bail out/recapitalize "systemic" banks. Anticipating this necessity, banks can feel free to engage in "moral hazard" behavior by recklessly financing risky projects. For the sovereign's failure to bail them out would result in the collapse not just of the banks, but of all those institutional investors which have deposited their wealth in the banks and have claims against them, e.g. local governments, pension funds etc., which would also collapse as a direct consequence. Banks are indebted to their creditors/ depositors, and it is in view of these creditors and their survival that banks must be deemed "systemic," meaning that they cannot be allowed to go under in any circumstance. So they are rescued, as they had good reason to expect, and their losses socialized.

However, this rescue operation has led to a fiscal crisis that has severely affected sovereigns. Spending hundreds of billions of fiscal revenues on buying up the banks' toxic assets causes budget gaps that now need to be filled by – banks! Banks enjoy a somewhat miraculous second-strike capability: After having contracted heavy losses from reckless investments, they are not only being saved from economic death, they emerge stronger than before, because the credit they supply is now much more in demand.[7] The sovereign has come to depend on them for credit after they have depended upon the sovereign for rescuing them and their creditors and claimants.

In "normal" times, banks are favorably disposed to financing sovereigns, because the latter have two options

---

[7] The Bank of International Settlements reported in March 2014 that between mid-2007 and mid-2013 the global total of sovereign debt has increased by 80 percent to 43 trillion US dollar, an amount which equals 59 percent of world GDP.

that private lenders do not enjoy. States used to be favored debtors because, first, they can *print* money if need be. Second, they can raise taxes to service their debt. For both these reasons, banks do not need to waste their capital to cover risk when dealing with states. But these options, which used to make state debtors attractive to banks, are no longer given in the Euro zone. First, not national central banks but only the ECB can "print" money. Banks also have reason to worry that printing money will cause inflation, and inflation will decrease the real value of the state's future debt payments. As to raising taxes, this option is also diminished in the Euro world. Why? Because with unrestricted capital mobility and in the absence of tax harmonization within the EU, higher (direct) taxes can easily be avoided through capital flight from the debtor state. What states would rather be inclined to do in the crisis, under conditions of inter-state tax competition as they prevail in the EU, is to *lower* (corporate) income-tax rates in order to attract or keep investors.[8] To the extent that states are no longer favored by banks as preferred borrowers, they have to pay the price of increased interest rates. In the absence of those two privileges it no longer enjoys, the only remaining way a state in need of credit can make itself credit-worthy to the banking industry is to cut those budgets destined for purposes other than debt service, such as infrastructure investment and social spending, thus assuring banks (in the short term, that is) of the ability to service debt.

---

[8] Whether or not such reduction of the corporate tax *rate* will actually attract more investment to a country and increase its tax *revenues* depends entirely on what "everyone else" is doing. If all states practice tax competition, it is investors that end up in the *tertius gaudens* position.

That these cuts will negatively affect current demand as well as future growth prospects of the state asking for credit does not, in itself, need to worry the banks. (We do not have clear indications as to what extent, if any, they worry about the social crisis and potential political instability which may result from harsh austerity measures.) But banks cannot fail to note that cuts of some kinds of public expenditures will lead to diminished growth prospects, to the perception of which they will rationally respond by imposing higher risk premia ("spreads") on their sovereign debtors.[9] This in turn will work to fulfill pessimistic anticipations by precipitating the risk of economic decline and *increasing* the ratio of debt to GDP due to the steeper decline of the latter relative to the decline of the former. Banks depend on the state's financial and political capacity to manage its economy in ways that generate a tax base that in turn allows it to service its debt. But that consideration may well be beyond the horizon of the bank's strategic calculations.

In order to break this doom loop between banks and states it is easily understood and widely accepted within the EU that a *banking union* is called for, i.e., a safety mechanism that protects states from the calamity of having ever again to bail out failing banks in the future.[10] A version of such a union, widely criticized for being overly

---

[9] The point that proponents of "Eurobonds" and other forms of debt mutualization within the Euro zone make is to stress the need to break this vicious circle.

[10] The horror of having to face this condition again is plain in the words of German finance minister Wolfgang Schäuble (2013): "If we ever again had to face a crisis like in 2008, what would be at stake is not just the market economy but the entire societal formation of western democracy." (Interview in *Süddeutsche Zeitung*, April 4, 2013; my translation.)

---

complex, insufficiently inclusive of the entire banking sector, illusionary as to the medium-term security it provides and inadequate as to the volume of its funding,[11] has in fact been adopted by the EU in December 2013. It provides for a buffer that supposedly will protect states and taxpayers from having to bail out failing banks in the future. To that end, they are to be supervised so as to stay out of "irresponsibly" risky investments or engage in excessive rates of leverage. Deposits are to be insured so as to avoid "runs" on the banks. And "rotten apples" among the banks are to be eliminated through a resolution mechanism that is to be financed (if in full only by 2026) out of a fund (of a bare 55 bn euros) to be accumulated by the banks themselves.

States vs the real economy. To the extent the state turns, as to its source of its finance, from a tax state into a debt state, this gradual change also changes its spending obligations, with the spending on growth and employment being crowded out by spending on the costs of credit. This happens in a context when (a) a return to (direct) taxation as the main source of finance is precluded by the tax competition between states which allows mobile wealth to pick the location that is fiscally most favorable to them and when (b) other states on whose contributions and credit guarantees the state in question depends for the sake of its budgetary stability makes these contributions conditional upon a policy of fiscal austerity and distributionally regressive "reforms." Both tax competition and austerity conditionality decimate the resources that this state is able to spend on programs for the promotion of growth and employment, as austerity is known to impact negatively on the tax base and positively on the ratio of total debt

---

[11] "A big bank collapse would dwarf the available resources," comments the *FT* (Barker 2013).

---

to GDP. Just as an illustration, Greece, obeying the conditionality of the Troika, had in 2013 a budget *surplus* which caused the ratio of total debt to GDP to *rise* from 156.9 percent (2012) to 175.7 percent due to the *decline* suffered in its GDP! In other words: Highly indebted states under externally imposed austerity pressure are forced to use their fiscal resources for purposes other than programs to enhance their tax base and hence become ever more credit-dependent – a doom loop that exacerbates the state's dependency upon the credit (instead of taxing) mode of finance. A type of measure that could break this loop is the often proposed (but vehemently resisted by "core" member states invoking the "moral hazard" argument) debt mutualization through Euro bonds and similar devices. It would also help to limit capital flight through the EU-wide harmonization of corporate taxes and/or to impose (temporary) limits on capital mobility – all of which would allow deeply indebted states to use their fiscal resources for purposes that can boost demand and expand their tax base and thus extricate themselves from a condition of self-propelling indebtedness. Also, favorable loans provided to private banks by the ECB might be made conditional on them financing private investment and consumption at sustainable rates rather than speculative investments and government bonds. Yet all of those remedies would have to be enacted not by intergovernmental treaties (as in the case of the Fiscal Compact) but by a supranational authority sufficiently legitimated to make decisions which involve significant redistributive effects.

States vs citizens. The less legitimate and effective supra-national crisis policies become, the more voters will turn away and withdraw their support from Europe-wide policies; yet the more they turn away, the slimmer the chances for remedial policies at the increasingly discredited European level. What *needs* to be done cannot be *accomplished* due to the lack of democratic support within member states, and what *can* be done is ineffective as a way out of the crisis and often will exacerbate it. The problem is one of "time inconsistency": The implementation of promising long-term strategies is obstructed by the failure of "presentist" electorates fixated on a short-term time horizon to grant them green light, unless political leaders can *persuade* their constituencies to adopt a more far-sighted perspective. Analogously, we can speak of "space inconsistency",[12] or irrational disposition of "localism" – the refusal of national constituencies to include seemingly "far away" countries and regions into the strategic calculation of policy making.[13] As political parties capitulate before the challenge of widening the horizon of their voters in time and space, they themselves become ever more similar to their voters in terms of symptoms of plainly irrational "presentism" and "localism."

It is exceedingly hard to believe that these various contradictions and doom loops can be legislated out of operation, as for example through the pious stipulation that "Member States shall avoid excessive government deficits."[14] It is worth repeating that if they strictly follow the stipulation, their debt burden relative to GDP

---

[12] Enderlein 2013b.

[13] An example is the euphoria with which in core countries the influx of skilled labor and its human capital from the periphery is celebrated as helping receiving countries overcome their skilled labor scarcities at very favorable conditions of training costs and labor costs. A full, less "localist" assessment would have to include the reverse side, namely the sending countries' loss of skilled labor that may well be a prerequisite for their economic recovery.

[14] TFEU article 126,1.

will actually *increase*! Given the weakness of the EU's policy competencies, which is due to its lack of democratic legitimacy as well as enforcement capacity, it is fair to conclude that the Euro has rendered European democratic capitalism more capitalist and less democratic. It has been instrumental in the transformation of markets being embedded in states to states being embedded in (financial) markets and rather defenselessly exposed to their contingencies.

One of the two key indicators by which a national economy's recovery from the crisis (or the opposite) is measured is the ratio of *sovereign debt to annual GDP*. The other is its *unit costs of labor*, a measure of an economy's competitiveness, defined as the ratio of real wages and non-wage costs of labor to productivity. As to the former, the following ambivalence applies: up to an (uncertain) limit and depending on the structure of expenditures from the state budget, increases in sovereign debt will help the economy grow through the supply of infrastructure etc. and the demand stabilization of transfer and public services. Yet, as the debt needs to be serviced through interest and repayment, "high" levels of debt diminish the state's capacity to boost growth through those kinds of expenditures; also, "high" debt will increase interest rates, endanger the state's solvency and threaten the viability of the common currency as well as the interests of creditors. On the other hand, "debt brakes" and other externally imposed austerity measures will hinder the growth-inducing effect of debt-financed state expenditures, threatening growth and leaving the economy worse off compared to a situation with more expansive debt. What makes things worse is that there is no calculus available that would allow policy makers to figure out an "optimal" way out of the dilemma.

Instead, any solution adopted will be one that reflects the power relations between the supranational actors primarily interested in rescuing the currency and national actors trying to promote domestic growth and employment.

The other key indicator, *unit costs of labor*, determines a member state's capacity to balance its exports and imports. In order to improve that balance for a country with a trade deficit, states can "normally" rely on policies such as exchange-rate manipulation of national currencies and subsidization of exports and import restrictions (duties, quotas). But the Common Market and the Euro are precisely designed, for the sake of economic "modernization," to abolish the "normal" sovereignty of states by banning those instruments from their policy tool box. As a consequence, unit cost of labor becomes the main remaining lever to be pulled in case a trade deficit is to be corrected. This can happen by increasing labor productivity and/or by decreasing real costs of labor. The former requires, among other things, public expenditures for training, R&D, and infrastructure, the latter the lowering of wages and wage-related social expenditures, such as pensions. In case a state fails to implement either of these for reasons of fiscal and/or political unfeasibility, its trade deficit tends to become chronic. If that is the case and a permanent excess of domestic absorption of resources over domestic production occurs, the trade deficit state *exports* capital corresponding to the financial assets that net exporters *to* that state acquire.[15]

---

[15] It used to be the case that, in order for one country to take control of the economy and polity of another country, the former

The Euro currency area is a highly heterogeneous one, among many other aspects in terms of real wage development and productivity. In spite of the built-in pressures to "modernize" and "converge," it is utterly unrealistic (and in no obvious sense desirable, at that) that at any time member-state economies will become similar in their competitiveness, meaning that current account deficits/surpluses would verge toward zero. For the Greek balance of external trade to equalize, Greek export items would have to become at least 40 percent less expensive in Euro terms. On the other side, German exports would have to be 20 percent more expensive in order to reduce that country's export surplus to zero.[16] (Incidentally, German export surplus for 2011 has been, relative to GDP, *twice* that of China.) Yet a balancing of international trade seems hardly conceivable, as neither Greek workers, pensioners, and political parties trying to defend their interests would allow this to happen, nor would German employers or any conceivable minister of finance.

Nevertheless, and given the massive advantages the German economy derives from the existence of the Euro, the prediction does not seem overly risky that

---

must *occupy* the latter by military means. This is no longer needed. Today one can have perfectly peaceful relations with a particular country and still largely control it – simply by appropriating more and more of its *economic* assets through running a permanent trade surplus and by destroying its *political* sovereignty by depriving the country (through austerity and "reform" conditionality and due to its high indebtedness) of its budgetary and other legislative autonomy. Whether by plan (as George Soros suggests) or as an unintended result, the outcome may be the creation of "a German empire with the periphery as its hinterland."
[16] Schäfer 2013.

---

any conceivable German government will do everything necessary to keep the common currency intact by avoiding the default of any member of the Euro club. (The emphasis is on *doing* everything (and being tacitly aware of the need to do so) – not on *saying* so and least of all *promising* to do so.) For this currency allows the German economy to live in an ideal world where pleasure is not followed by regret, meaning that an export surplus is not followed, and its continuation thus limited, by the appreciation of the currency of the country. As there is no longer a "national" currency, the export surplus becomes sustainable endlessly, if only at the expense of others. The only thing that needs to happen is for the export surplus country to finance the deficit of the losers or, failing that, due to domestic political resistance to any debt mutualization, to force trade deficit countries of the Euro zone to adopt measures of "reform," of internal devaluation (through the cutting of wages and transfers) and of austerity. However, as all these measures are politically resisted in the deficit countries and will not conceivably help to revitalize the trading position of Euro countries suffering from an export deficit, the difference in their unit costs of labor that favors the net exporters and inflicts damage and misery on the net importers must be narrowed from the other side: Not by bringing unit costs further down in the periphery but by bringing them *up* in the core! Rather than financing other countries' trade deficits and/or forcing them into counterproductive internal devaluation, Germany, the global extreme case of an export surplus economy, has a strong interest in internal *re*valuation of its labor and public sectors, meaning an increase in infrastructure investment and public services, the strengthening of consumer demand through wage increases, and the raising of both minimum wages and maximum income and wealthtax rates. While all of these measures would decrease the German labor cost and export advantage (which partly derives from the installation of a low-wage sector through the infamous Hartz IV laws of 2005), they would help to compensate for some of the periphery's trade disadvantage by improving their opportunities to sell export goods to German consumers and to benefit from the labor demand caused by German infrastructure investment. Most importantly perhaps, they would replace the political fear in the surplus country of having to pay for "them" with the political attraction of serving "us" (while improving, as a side effect, the capacity of the deficit countries to sell their goods and services abroad). As American observers such as the prominent trade expert Fred Bengsten[17] have argued, Germany must and eventually will cease to pursue its vital interest in the preservation of the common currency through financing the deficit of the losers alone; instead, it will turn to a (domestically as well as within the Euro zone) much more popular strategy of *internal* adjustment, its self-transformation into a less export-addicted economy. Rather than forcing cuts of wages and pensions in Greece and elsewhere at great costs in terms of political integration, why not increase wages and public spending in Germany and other core countries to the economic and political benefit of the EU as a whole?[18]

---

[17] Oral communication, Berlin, June 10, 2014.

[18] In this sense, Andrew Watt (2014) and others have given the German Coalition Agreement of November 2013 an optimistic reading, suggesting that it implicitly follows a logic of "Good for Germany can be good for Europe." http://www.social-europe.eu/2013/11/german-coalition-agreement/

4

No Return to
Square One

In addition to being built on the "wrong" currency area and being endowed with insufficient policy capacities, there is a third flaw: the Euro currency is, for all practical purposes, an *irreversible* arrangement. I would defend this (controversial) view with two arguments. First, the complexities and risks involved in a return to national currencies, the splitting up of the Euro zone into two or more currency zones or the unilateral withdrawal of members (e.g. by "Grexit") from the zone are of an uncontrollable and prohibitive order of magnitude. The risks involved in an exit or breakup are feared to affect all members of the zone (as well as their banking sectors). Second, partly as a consequence of these risks and complexities and partly for other reasons, none of the present participants in the Euro zone (neither in the north nor in the south, and neither at the elite nor the mass level) has a clear and overwhelming *interest* in abandoning the Euro.[1] As to the first point, the abolition of the Euro cannot possibly be envisaged as an

[1] The extent to which the common currency and the common market have already propelled the division of labor can only be reversed at great and unknown costs. Today, it has become a

overnight surprise operation. Actually, it would be an unprecedented operation for which no legal procedures in the Treaties exist. While article 50 of the TEU describes the procedure for a member state that wishes to leave the EU, there is no way for a country to leave the Euro zone yet stay in the EU. The moment such a move is even proposed publicly, owners of financial assets would have sufficient time to convert them into other currencies in order to escape anticipated losses. If one country were to exit, banks holding government bonds would have cause to anticipate that other countries will follow suit, which is exactly what would have to happen if banks started to speculate against the next candidate(s). If the renationalization of currencies of all current Euro zone members were to happen as a simultaneous move, no less than 153 exchange rates between the eighteen Euro countries would have to be fixed at the same point in time. Or a system of time-limited parallel currencies would have to be established that would be vulnerable to all kinds of non-cooperative gaming.

Even if it were widely agreed by member states that the introduction of the Euro into a fundamentally flawed currency zone was a huge mistake, the same applies by now simply to *undoing* that mistake. Legally, part of the commitments the new member states made at the point of their accession was a promise to transform their economies in ways that made them viable, as prescribed by the Maastricht criteria, as members of the Euro zone. In return, they were endowed with the entitlement to

---

gross distortion to describe an Audi car as a "German" product; this is as untrue as it would be to describe a GM car as a "Michigan" product. In both cases, the component parts of the product are manufactured in many locations, for the coordination of which a single currency is a virtual *conditio sine non*.

---

financial aid from EU funds, which supposedly (yet so far widely unrealistically) would help them boost productivity and competitiveness of their national economies along a trajectory of "cohesion" and "convergence." If these mutual commitments were to be suspended, an avalanche of adverse economic consequences would be triggered: the renationalization of monetary policy would allow periphery countries to devalue their currency yet leave them all the more deeply in trouble with the challenge of servicing the Euro-denominated debt they have accumulated. Also, private sector financial lenders would immediately increase their pressure ("spreads") on member states that have not yet left the Euro, thus causing the incalculable costs of a domino effect that eventually would also threaten the economy of the trade surplus countries because they would lose substantial parts of their export markets. Moreover, leaving the Euro would force leavers also to leave the regulatory regime of European law, as compliance with its rules would instantaneously become unaffordable to them. The dissolution of the Euro zone and, as an inescapable medium-term consequence, the EU would be equivalent to a tsunami of economic as well as political regression.

Even more decisive is the second argument as to why the Euro has passed a point of no return: Strange though this may seem, Europeans of both the trade surplus and the trade deficit countries are united in having a rational interest in holding fast to the Euro once they have adopted it, some electorally effective yet policy-irrelevant populist appeals notwithstanding. A simple cross-tabulation of the *opportunities* provided by the Euro and the *risks* to be anticipated from its breakdown, both in the perception of the *core* and *periphery* countries' economic and political elites yields the following picture.

The core's opportunities: Core countries benefit, directly and indirectly, from the Euro, including from the imbalances, divergences, and economic crisis it has caused in the periphery, in several ways. One is the inflow of cheap capital seeking safe financial investment outlets in the core. Another is the undervalued external exchange rate of the Euro, which allows net exporters to stay in that position also in their trade with non-EU partners. Surplus countries of the core (such as Germany) would see the external value of their new Deutschmark shoot through the roof, thus decimating their exports and export-driven growth potential. Also, the extremely cheap credit that the ECB indiscriminately makes available to all Euro states benefits the budgetary balance of the surplus countries. As seen by the surplus countries, the maintenance of the Euro is an asset because it ties the hands of national monetary policy makers in deficit countries and makes foreign investment more predictable and immune from monetary defense measures taken by them. For all these reasons the core's economic and political elites are firmly committed to rescue and defend the Euro, as at least some business elites of member states currently outside the Euro zone are still eager to join in. Accordingly, they have excellent reasons to incur some "sacrifices" in order to defend the currency.

The core's risks: If others were to exit the Euro, peripheral economies would cease to be able, due to devaluation, to import what the core wants to export. Commercial prudence alone advises against letting prospective customers go under. Also, as one periphery country would leave, financial markets would start to speculate against others in the periphery, thus triggering an uncontrollable dynamic of self-fulfilling anticipation that also would put the core's banks at risk. To be sure, voters in core countries may be mobilized against the Euro and the sharing of burdens and risks that its defense involves. Yet to convince "northern" voting publics that burden sharing (with harsh conditionalist strings attached, of course) is still an acceptable idea, the argument may work that *failing* to do so might be even *more* expensive;[2] this argument has so far mostly served its purpose. It is an entirely prudential argument, not one from solidarity obligations. The banking industry will warmly welcome such anxiety-driven acts of supra-national risk-sharing as it has been institutionalized in the ESM.

The periphery's risks: In the absence of the Euro and after their return to national currencies, the new money would have to be significantly devalued while their debt burden (denominated in Euros) would become significantly heavier, causing an immediate default with its catastrophic economic consequences within respective countries. Devaluation would not just lead to exports becoming cheaper, but imports more expensive. Depending on the price elasticity of imported goods, the latter effect will come with the risk of inflation that is likely to destroy the initial export advantage. In order to fight inflation and to fight the flight of capital, interest rates would have to move up, with an equally unwelcome impact for economic recovery. For these and related reasons, even troubled Euro member states, as well as their trading partners within the zone, have equally strong reasons to opt for staying in the monetary union.

The periphery's opportunities: In view of the rational aversion of the core to the dissolution of the single currency, staying in the Euro zone (in spite of the massive social and *economic* pains it has inflicted on periphery

---

[2] Bertelsmann-Stiftung 2012.

countries already) can be considered to be an asset, as it provides them with some *political* leverage at the European level. As core countries are aware of the risk of contagion and a possible yet incalculable domino effect caused by one deficit country's exit, the fear of core countries that this might happen can serve as a lever for a deficit country to extract assistance and concessions from the core.[3] The devaluation of a leaver's new national currency against the Euro would increase its debt burden, making it immediately insolvent – at the peril of international banks holding its bonds. Another potential asset would become manifest if deficit countries managed to join forces (as Monti and Rajoy in fact successfully did at the June 2012 summit), using their political resources in the EC, EP, the Council, the Commission, the ECB, the European media and trade union federations etc. in opposing counter-productive austerity policies and demanding major concessions from their counterparts, such as sovereign debt mutualization and a *direct* engagement of the rescue fund ESM with troubled banks. As Euro zone membership provides them with an arena to which they would not have access any longer after leaving the single currency, this arena can arguably be used, more than has been done so far, to voice demands jointly, extract resources, and politicize the flaws of the EU's institutional setup. After all, if banks can extract resources from states by hinting at the fact that they are "systemic," so probably can states. It is a puzzle (to which I admit not having a fully plausible answer) why political elites as well as non-elites of deficit countries have so far failed to undertake joint and vigorous efforts to push the alternative frame of "being systemic." While players in the

---

[3] Gammelin and Löw 2014: 25.

"Germany" position often take the paternalist position of claiming superior knowledge about what is good for those in the "Greek" position, the latter players might well respond by turning the tables and by telling and trying to convince the former about what is, in a medium-term perspective, good for *them*. No such political leverage (nor even the economic transfers their Euro zone and EU membership entitles them to) would be available to them any longer after their exit.[4] These considerations help to make sense of the seemingly paradoxical Eurostat finding that, while support for the *EU* is declining as a consequence of the crisis, scare-induced support for the *Euro* in countries of the currency zone is consistently going *up* (except for Ireland where it was still at a high level of 72 percent in 2013).

Thus, all members of the Euro zone (as well as the eight still outside, which are, with the exception of the UK, Denmark, and (so far) Sweden, committed to and preparing to join at some future point) seem rationally united in their strategic interests to keep the Euro alive. To be sure, in a number of countries on both sides of the divide anti-Euro political parties and movements have formed, demanding the abolition of the Euro. Yet they seem unlikely to gain (beyond their impact on national *politics*) a decisive role in the making of *policy* as devised by the governments of member states or at the level of European supranational policy. Nor are national majorities of non-elites anywhere disposed to exit the Euro, much though they have reason to complain about the damages it has caused.

In sum, even if the technical problems of a currency re-conversion could be handled, both sides of the new European divide would stand to lose from it and would

---

[4] Tsoukalis 2014: 60–1.

therefore resist it. *The Euro, in short, is a mistake the undoing of which would be an even greater mistake,* as seen by all participants. The original mistake consists in the fact that the common currency *presupposes* for its viability a considerable degree of economic *homogeneity* of the currency zone, at least effective tools to *promote* convergence and to make hopes for convergence credible; yet it *causes* by its operation and due to the absence of European fiscal, economic, and social policy making competencies a *widening divergence* between participants. But in spite of its divisiveness, the Euro is a monetary regime the maintenance of which is rationally supported, if for very different reasons, by its winners and losers alike. The irreversibility of Europe's lop-sided integration suggests that the so far highly deficient machinery for supranational policy making must be completed rather than demolished, particularly as it is an indispensable (if in its current structure ill-designed) device for overcoming the crisis and providing Europe with measures to prevent its repetition.

5

In Search of Political Agency

In the history of the EU, it was widely believed that an "ever closer" integration will be driven by emerging necessities that lead European elites to find incremental *ad hoc* solutions without stirring up much attention or mobilizing demands for participation and representation on the part of European citizens. Whenever a friction comes up, it will be (and in fact often has been) dealt with, according to neofunctionalist integration theory, through the inconspicuous and quasi-spontaneous stepping up of sovereignty transfers and emergent new modes of cooperation needed to avoid negative spill-over effects.[1] In a step-by-step fashion, integration will generate societal actors who pave the road to more integration, making the whole process halting but irreversible. The legitimacy this mode of the integration process requires is of the "output" variety, earned by technocratic decision makers through their ongoing production of relatively uncontroversial and

---

[1] The classical source is Haas 1961.

inconspicuous policies made "for" the people yet in no plausible sense "by" it.

The current banking and associated Euro, fiscal and economic crises are the first instances in the history of the EU where this logic no longer applies. Member state governments are no longer ready to transfer sovereignty, pool resources, and practice cooperation to the extent that appears "functionally" necessary. Confidence in the quasi-automatic adaptation of a neofunctionalist sort and its basis in the "permissive consensus" of constituencies is no longer warranted. The stakes involved have grown too high for that, and, instead of the neofunctionalist auto-pilot, "real" agency needs to step in and to engage in "political" (i.e., strategic, resourceful and contested rather than adaptive) action.

The crisis condition itself raises very basic issues concerning the further viability of the integration that has been reached so far and the desirability of its continuation. As policy decisions on crisis management involve issues of redistribution and conflicting claims on resources, the conflicting interests of stakeholders must be processed through an institutional machinery generating "input" legitimacy through democratic procedures. The key question is where such political agency might come from and what might inspire it. On the other hand: What a (currently shrinking) minority of EU enthusiasts among elites and non-elites would dream of for many years in terms of deepening the integration process, has suddenly, under the impact of the crisis and also under the threatening impact of growing political forces of Rightist populism threatening to demolish the unfinished integration project, turned into an urgent rescue operation that makes the building of fiscal and economic governing capacities at the EU level a plain imperative. In what follows, I shall review a number of answers to that question. Can it be the intrinsic commitment of Europeans to further the project of deeper political integration? Can it be an alliance of major political forces and long-term economic interests that will inspire a vigorous and widely supported strategy to end the crisis? Can it be the agency coming out of the institutional repertoire the EU has acquired so far – the ECB, the EC, the Commission, the EP? Or can it perhaps be the determined and benevolent leadership of one or a small group of countries willing to take responsibility for the building of a post-crisis EU?

The elections for the EP of May 2014 have not resulted in anything like a clear pattern of agency. Instead, there are two sets of worrying outcomes, one substantive and the other procedural. The substantive outcome is the vast increase of Rightist populist votes and the new strength of a variety of Rightist anti-European voices in the EP. Gains of the respective parties were strongest in France (with the triumph of *Front National*), the UK (with that of *UKIP*) and Denmark. Proponents of EU integration may derive some comfort from the fact that these parties all engage in (negative) *politics* of rejection and protest without having much of a shared *policy* or strategic vision on how the economic and institutional crises might be overcome other than by calling for withdrawal and exit. Moreover, Rightist populists have notorious difficulties of forming alliances among themselves, to say nothing about forming an alliance with Syriza-type Leftist critics of EU integration policies. Nevertheless, a vigorous politics of obstruction is to be expected from these forces that pro-European party groups within the EP will have to withstand by forming an alliance on key policy and reform decisions or, if failing to do so due to the temptation of right-of-center parties of the EPP alliance, to outcompete the far

Right by steps towards timid self-assimilation, have to face stagnation and paralysis.[2] Also, it is striking that the countries with the highest increases in right-wing anti-European shares of the vote are in no way those, with the limited exception of Greece, hit hardest by the debt crisis and its social devastations. To the contrary, the Right became or remained strong in the core, including, in addition to the three countries just mentioned, Germany, Finland, Austria and, with some qualification, the Netherlands. This suggests that popular fears have been an important factor in these countries – be it the economic fear of having to foot the bill for other Euro zone members' debt and/or the cultural fear of inward migration from other EU member states and/or the political fear of the specter of "foreign rule" originating from "Brussels." Rightist populists object to the EU and Euro zone policies not because they inflict misery and unemployment but because they are (or might become) overly generous in terms of transnational burden-sharing and excessively liberal concerning mobility rights. Another notable substantive outcome is the evidence that, without a single exception, the eleven post-Communist new member states show turnout rates that are (often far)[3] below the (unweighted) EU average of 43%; for electorates in these countries, issues of European integration seem still to be largely a remote side show.

As to the procedural outcome, a tangle has resulted from the election outcome that consists in three

---

[2] If such inertia of a centrist alliance between PES and EPP suffering from "grand coalition" symptoms is to be avoided, all depends on the capacity of the Green and united Left party groups in the EP to provide the socialist and social democratic bloc with an offer of credible and viable cooperation.

[3] The extreme case being Slovakia with a turnout of just 13%.

---

overlapping cleavages. While the election campaign was based on the duel, to be democratically decided by voters, of *Spitzenkandidaten* nominated by EU-wide *party* alliances of center-left *vs*. center-right parties, the immediate aftermath of the election saw the rise of an *inter-institutional* cleavage (EC *vs*. EP), which in turn was driven by a cleavage of *member states* (with the UK and others being opposed to either of the candidates for the Commission presidency). Taken together, the substantive and institutional outcomes and patterns of conflict of the 2014 EP elections do not forebode well for the democratic quality and legitimacy of European policy-making of the European Parliament and its capacity for agency.

6
Finalitées: Bases of Identification with European Integration as a Political Project

After the crisis and the frustrations, divisions, conflicts, and suffering it has caused, why should the integration project of an "ever closer union" be robustly deemed desirable any longer at the mass level? Why should there be a mass perception of Europe as a "project" intrinsically worth pursuing and making sacrifices for in the name of some transnational identity that nurtures a sense of belonging and duties of solidarity in a community constituted by law rather than national or religious identity? Among intellectuals, it has become *chic* to display a sense of sobriety (if not cynicism) that has overcome all misplaced "Europhoria," most legitimately applying to the claim of a European "identity" deriving from some notion of the "Christian Occident," which is a plain non-starter if suggested as a self-description of the most secularized region of the globe. One answer to this key question of sufficiently motivated and adequately resourceful agency might of course be that "the Europeans," the citizens of the EU themselves, elites and (majorities of) non-elites alike, are sufficiently committed and interested to do (or allow to be done) "whatever it takes" to overcome the crisis by deepening integration.

The various goals, aspirations, and guiding visions ("*Leitbilder*") potentially driving the integration process make up a set of moving targets, with diverse priorities pursued by (groups of) member states. These aspirations are of seven different kinds, which are in no way mutually exclusive. I shall first describe them briefly and then proceed to point to some developments that seem to undermine their motivational force.

(1) European integration has accomplished and can guarantee for future *international peace*. This includes the neutralization of German prevalence and the transformation of "German Europe" into a "European Germany" before the backdrop of memories and legacies of the two world wars. Europe is to be credited with its achievement "to render Germany harmless"[1] through the consolidation of peace and cooperation between France and Germany. A related aspiration that has driven European integration was the perceived mission of Western Europe to prevail in the Cold War.

(2) Europe as the continuously redeemed promise of *economic* prosperity *cum* social *inclusion*. Here, the motivating assumption is that full market integration through the four freedoms promises to yield prosperity gains through economies of scale (compensating for Europe's liability of consisting of mostly "small" states) and enhanced competition and productivity gains, complemented by the common currency that reduces transaction costs in border-crossing commerce and production, promotes the international division of labor, provides calculability tying the hands of national monetary policy

---

[1] Marsh 2013: 1.

makers, thus freeing the European economy from the monetary rule of the German Bundesbank.

(3) Europe as an institutionalized commitment to protect and promote representative and *democratically accountable government* and rule of law as its basic standard of legitimate political organization designed to protect the freedom of European citizens.

(4) United Europe as an agent in *international* politics with the ambition of achieving a role for united Europe (as a "soft power" counterweight to US "hard" power) in global international relations and of protecting European polities, economies, and societies, in spite of manifold forms of Atlantic cooperation, from becoming fully dominated by American interests and norms.

(5) Europe as the globally unique scene of intrinsically valuable diversity of cultures, historical traditions, artistic styles, languages, patterns of settlement, and urban structures, all of which stand in a relationship of mutual exchange and influence.

(6) Europe as an "auto-paternalist" supranational arrangement of mutual supervision and control. EU institutions performing such supervision and control are needed because of dangerous legacies (of xenophobic sentiments, aggressive nationalist attitudes, chauvinistic confrontation with neighboring nations, religious wars, authoritarian temptations, imperial ambitions, corrupt political authorities, etc.), which are "bad habits" engrained in the histories and "cultural genes" of Europeans. To counter this regressive potential, the institutions of integrated Europe must and can perform the role of a *mission civilisatrice interne* by safeguarding the rule of law, enforcing human and civil rights, organizing encounters with other Europeans and their histories and guaranteeing minimal standards of "good governance" and rule of law. Europe's capacity for

self-monitoring reflexivity may itself be a reflection of European history.[2] Some years before the crisis, I tried out a perhaps overly daring argument: European history in the modern age, comprising its history of *events* as well as its history of *ideas*, can be conceived of:

> as the coincidence in space of the worst crimes and aberrations *and* the most elaborate and explicit normative standards by which they must be condemned as such. Throughout its modern history, Europe has plentifully supplied itself with the "real" objects of its self-critical normative scrutiny. Due to this perplexing coincidence of opposites, the *self-critical appreciation* of the wrongs that have been committed by European nations (from the crusades to colonial rule to the Holocaust) in their own history is arguably distinctively European. This capacity and propensity for self-revision and *autocritique* has no parallel, as far as I can see, in any of the non-European civilizations, e.g. those of the United States, China, or Japan.[3]

As virtually all European nation states have, in their historical traditions and present-day cultural patterns, evidently durable propensities to violate basic standards of civility, the capacity of Europe to control these pro-

---

[2] The balanced coexistence and mutual integration of conflicting structures and countervailing principles has arguably been a driving aspiration in specifically European social and political thought. This could be illustrated by the uses made in European intellectual history of a myriad of pairs of concepts, such as Church and state, *Gemeinschaft* and *Gesellschaft*, household and enterprise, work and leisure, law and morality, market and state, *bourgeois* and *citoyen*, labor and capital, system and life world, use value and exchange value, social justice and market justice, European and national identity, *demos* and *ethnos* etc.

[3] Offe 2006.

pensities in an, as it were, "auto-paternalist" fashion, must be valued quite highly. For instance, propensities, temptations, and just conventional habits of majorities to discriminate against minorities and of male-operated institutions against women, of civil servants to enrich themselves by taking bribes from clients or to embezzle public funds, of owners of large enterprises ("oligarchs") to control the conduct of public policy and courts of justice, of governments to interfere with the freedom of press of oppositional media or of religious elites to control legislation, of public authorities to neglect or mistreat refugees and asylum seekers or to deny the disadvantaged minimal poor relief and health services, of police forces to engage in brutal uses of violence – all of these and many other kinds of violations, including military violence of armed groups or authoritarian regression of national regimes, are by no means categorically absent in EU-Europe; they are just considerably less likely to occur, or occur without being sanctioned, than they are virtually everywhere outside of the EU. To the extent this is – and remains – true, the EU must be seen as a normatively valuable asset of mutual monitoring, supervision, and control of its citizens and member states which, I submit, is superior in its direct effects and standard-setting capacities to what member states would be able to accomplish by their own means.

(7) Finally, the thinnest and most defensive argument for strengthening European integration is this: Europe-wide institutions as representing the only adequate scope of managing Europe-wide problems.[4] It is better, for the time being, to have an insufficient and democratically

---

[4] A metaphor is that if you need to fight a fire on the upper floors of a high-rise building, you need a *long* ladder. "National" means of intervention are simply far too "short".

---

questionable institutional machinery in place (including the ECB and the ECJ) than no machinery at all. The crisis may even function as a challenge to develop the EU's democratic qualities as the latter become necessary to cope with it. As the crisis itself is Europe-wide, so must the institutional apparatus be, in order to come up with effective and durable solutions to the crisis.

Taken together, these self-ascribed missions and (partial) accomplishments of the EU as an historically unique supra-national non-state form a grand narrative supplying it with legitimacy and normative validity. The components of this narrative, however, can be put to an often sobering empirical test as to their validity and continuing motivational force. As to (1), the memory of integrating Europe as a *peace-making agency* and its accomplishment of Franco-German cooperation has largely sunk into the mist of the past. It is to be taken for granted already, not something to be achieved by or credited to the EU. Today, international peace in Europe (if less so *intra*-national cohesion and integrity of EU member states such as the UK, Belgium, Spain, and Ireland!) appears as a condition that can be taken for granted (also, and particularly so in the eyes of new member states in CEE, thanks to NATO, not the EU). Yet while having been successful in consolidating peaceful relations among its member states, it has spectacularly failed, contrary to the ambitions of its "neighborhood policies," to enforce international peace in its eastern neighborhood (Ukraine, Georgia, Moldova, Azerbaijan) and, in particular, southern neighborhood across the Mediterranean and the MENA region. In the Balkans, peace-making through ending the post-Yugoslav wars has been critically contingent on the role played by the USA and NATO.

Item (2) has lost much of its legitimating significance as the prosperity market-integrated Europe has managed to generate is very unevenly distributed across member states, regions, and social classes, with all these divisions being massively exacerbated by the uncontrolled dynamics of the EMU and the chain of crises it has triggered or failed to control. Moreover, prosperity and growth (to the overall declining extent that it takes place at all, in the "real" economy of Europe, that is) has come at the price of tax competition among member states, labor market liberalization and social dumping, social expenditure freezes and often retrenchments, stagnating wages, record levels of overall unemployment, and growing precariousness of working and living conditions. In the absence of welfare state remedies instituted at the EU level itself, this leaves entire social classes and generations considerably less protected ("included"), more vulnerable to the repercussions of the financial market and debt crisis, and overall worse off than they were behind the borders of their national welfare states, which are now exposed to competitive pressures to cut labor costs. The once widely shared self-description of Europe being on its way to a fully realized ESM (the European Social Model, comprising steady growth, inclusive prosperity, and democratic codetermination and contrasting itself with the untamed/uncoordinated Anglo-Saxon capitalism of the "American way of life") has been thoroughly replaced by the other ESM (the European Stability Mechanism, its plain opposite, with harsh austerity conditionalism attached to it). Europe no longer simply represents a credible promise of neither greater nor ever more fairly distributed prosperity, least of all for a socio-economic convergence of old and new member states or that between core and peripheral regions and countries. On the other hand, the possibility cannot be categorically excluded that, under the social impact of the crisis and the suffering it has caused, the "social dimension" of the EU is to be revived.[5] Welfare states that have in part been demolished at the national level can, in response to concerted political struggles originating from the deficit countries and by deconstructing the deceptive "subsidiarity" tale and the fictitious nature of "sovereignty claims" of member states, be rebuilt at the EU level. Such de-/reconstruction would also help to activate the interest of national constituencies in and political engagement with European politics. Yet, for the time being, the forces and strategies that would stand for a credible project to build an EU-wide *"social"* market economy and welfare state are simply not in sight; on the contrary, European (predominantly "negative") integration has been causally responsible for welfare state retrenchment, labor market liberalization and growing precariousness.

As to (3) the *democratic* appeal of European integration, it is clearly blemished by the post-democratic[6] experience within member states, the "democratic deficit" of the EU itself, and the corruption of and disenchantment with liberal democracy as a regime form prevailing not exclusively, but most drastically in several of the new (post-Communist) member states that have joined the EU in 2004 and 2007, respectively. With less than a handful of exceptions (among them Luxemburg and Germany), satisfaction with democracy, trust in political elites, and support for democracy have all declined from 2007 to 2011 – most dramatically so in Greece (with support down by 42.7 percent), Spain (30.7 percent) and Cyprus (19.9 percent). [7] In contrast to the hopes and aspirations

---

[5] Cf. Andor 2013a, b.
[6] Crouch 2004.
[7] Armingeon and Guthmann 2013.

---

expressed by many of the "Euromaidan" activists of Ukraine in early 2014, being part of the EU and undergoing further integration is hardly experienced by the citizens of member states as a gain in terms of their equal liberty and other qualities of democracy. To the contrary, the EU is widely perceived as a political entity that *deprives* the familiar institutions of national democracy of some of their democratic content. As to the rule-of-law component of liberal democracy, it must be said that the giant scope of violations of privacy and freedom of communication committed by a cartel of state actors (such as NSA) and private corporations (Google etc.) have further damaged its normative appeal.

As to (4), the Common Foreign and Security Policy along with the European Neighborhood Policy is so far an incipient construction site for the accomplishments of which the EU can hardly claim much internal credit and support. Also, with two of the EU member states being nuclear powers, members of the UNSC and, together with Spain and Portugal, the world's largest systems of post-colonial ties and responsibilities, a coordinated and distinctive European (as opposed to member states' national or NATO dominated) foreign and security policy is hard to envision. The consistent failure of the EU to prevent or reconcile international as well as domestic conflicts in both its eastern neighborhood and the entire MENA region and to contribute to the stabilization of these regions is hardly inspiring visions about the EU's role in international politics.

Concerning (5), "diversity" as an intrinsically valuable quality of Europe, there are a number of doubts about the concept itself as well as the role appeals to "diversity" can play as a motivating force. First of all, diversity (of languages, artistic traditions, urban patterns, religious beliefs, economic institutions, historical traditions) is a *fact*, not a *value*; "diversity could never be a value of the same kind as liberty, equality or fraternity."[8] Secondly, we may be well advised to distinguish between "diversity as plurality" and diversity as deviance or even division. That is to say, some diversities (e.g. "cultural" ones in the broadest sense) deserve to be respected and protected, while this is not as obviously the case with others, e.g. those of levels of corruption or poverty or the division between the core and the periphery in the EU. There are simply many different kinds of differences subsumed under "diversity." But people also differ on where to draw the line between "worthy" and "unworthy" diversities. Allegedly, there are places in Europe where the use of olive oil for cooking in apartment buildings is considered something *not* to be tolerated by proprietors as the smell (and its ethnic connotations) can diminish the real estate value of buildings. Thirdly, it is not clear how European integration can or does contribute in significant ways (i.e., beyond the annual naming of "cultural capitals" etc.) in the protection of diversity, except for the guarantees of rights of ethnic and linguistic minorities – an accomplishment that belongs to my point (6). It might well be argued[9] that European integration is, at least in some areas,[10] eroding rather than protecting diversity. It is not clear that the appeal to diversity as a motivating foundation of European identity is more than a fad of postmodernist or romanticizing intellectuals.

---

[8] Anderson 2009: 527.
[9] As does Giorgio Agamben (2013) when calling for defense of a "Latin" *vs* an intrusively homogenizing "Germanic" culture.
[10] Such as the debate on whether the traditional Spanish time regime with its mid-day *siesta* should be abolished; cf. Yardley (2014).

As to (6), the role of European integration as a precautionary safeguard against de-civilizing tendencies which sets and enforces standards of civil and human rights everywhere in the Union, in particular the protection of minority rights, is an institutional asset that cannot lightly be dismissed. Whether or not one can be satisfied with the mixed success with which the EU has enforced these standards (as they apply, for instance, to recent constitutional changes in Hungary) is not at issue here. My point is that human rights violations such as the use of torture and massive breaches of privacy as they have been introduced in the USA under Bush Jr (and have continued under President Obama) cannot be envisaged to go undetected and unsanctioned in today's Europe. But this modest conceptualization of Europe's "mission" is about something to be *prevented*, not something (beyond the unconditional rule of law) to be *achieved*. Moreover, such prevention is most effective at the point of accession (which can be conditionally denied – the case of Turkey), while being much more difficult to implement once EU-membership has been granted.

The normatively least ambitious but perhaps (precisely for that reason) most widely accepted argument in support of European integration is the remaining consideration (7) that after the chosen course of European monetary integration has led Europeans into such perilous territory, Europeans need to join forces and intensify their cooperation in order to extricate themselves from the troubles they have jointly caused. A rigorous renationalization of monetary and economic policy making would plunge Europe back into the "state of nature" of a huge negative sum game among states. Again, this is a defensive or "preventative" kind of argument, unlikely to mobilize action; its persuasiveness depends on the perceived validity of the counter-factual (i.e., international anarchy after a disintegration of the EU and renationalization of member states) on which it is based. The other remaining argument (admittedly a "thin" and entirely defensive one, though symptomatically often invoked these days) is basically an argument *e contrario*: Europe, its present state and future steps of integration, and even the EMU must be defended because the costs, uncertainties, and incalculable collateral damages of its falling apart are to be feared foremost because of their prohibitive magnitude. Along these lines, Fritz Scharpf[11] has undertaken a (quasi) cost-benefit analysis, suggesting that the "costs of non-disintegration" may be, after all, not quite as high as those of disintegration (that he refrains to specify). This result, however, as he rightly points out, hinges entirely on the accounting frame chosen as well as the "presently dominant beliefs" and evaluations. Should these beliefs undergo a re-framing, chances are that the price for unraveling the EU can be made to appear tolerable.

Summarizing what we can learn from this balance sheet of integration-related normative arguments about the EU's *finalitées*, it seems safe to conclude that the EU depends on receiving more loyalty and support from its citizens than it has been able to generate. Not only have the arguments "for" Europe lost force but also the arguments "against" (or disappointments with the EU and how it has performed in the crisis) gained in political strength. Positive answers to the Eurostat question concerning "support for Europe" have decreased on average of EU-27 from 48 to 31 percent, with the steepest drops registered in Greece (47 – 16), Portugal (55 – 22), Spain (59 – 26) and Italy (49 – 26). In 2007, 15 percent held

---

[11] Scharpf 2014.

---

negative views of the EU; by 2013 that number has almost doubled to 28 percent. There is not a single member state where trust in the EU has not declined in this period.[12] The EU and its further integration does not mobilize agency, invite engagement, or inculcate the notion of a "project" based on a widely shared sense of "identity" with its corollary of obligations of "solidarity" deriving from some "fellow-feeling." In short, the European Union does not do what nation states can do. On the contrary, there are many signs suggesting that under the impact of the crisis the dividing lines separating EU member states (both the East–West divides and the North–South divides) have deepened, and perceptions of a positive-sum game transformed into a zero-sum frame. The new complaint on both sides is that Brussels favours "the other side" in the conflict between center and periphery; it is a "clash between the democratic wills of citizens in northern and southern Europe." "Citizens in the creditor countries have become resistant to taking responsibility for the debts of others," while in the debtor countries European authorities' demands for comprehensive domestic reforms means that "Eurocrats have crossed many of the red lines of national sovereignty" and "emptied their national democracies of content."[13] Both debtors *and* creditors feel victimized by "Brussels," and there are no supranational political parties that could bridge the gap and decide on solutions. As a consequence, the net support of the EU – the percentage of national constituencies who trust and support the EU minus the percentage of those who distrust and reject it – has been sharply declining in the period 2007 to 2012: from +10 to –22 in France, from +30 to –22 in Italy, from

---

[12] Leonard and Torreblanca 2013.
[13] Ibid.

+42 to −52 in Spain, with the only exception to this trend being Bulgaria,[14] where the national political institutions are so intensely distrusted by the population that the EU fares moderately well in comparison.

The EU does not have a widely appealing and inspiring vision of its own future or that of its citizens to offer. That is of course not to deny the fact that not only investors and commercial elites, but also university students, as well as arts, media and professional elites are strongly appreciative of the opportunities integrated Europe affords to them. It is just to say that there is little reason to assume that the appreciation of Europe and its integration on the part of these elite segments will "trickle down" and eventually become a mass phenomenon inspiring a sense of inclusive solidarity among fellow-Europeans comparable to that which can be mobilized within the primary reference unit of the nation state.[15]

---

[14] Ibid.

[15] The ways in which Europeans cope effectively with their dilemma of their "dual citizenship," i.e., of being citizens of member states *and* at the same time citizens of the Union, varies widely across member states. For instance, among twenty European countries surveyed, Germans show the lowest percentage (except for Moldavians) of being "very proud" (20 percent) to belong to their nation and the highest percentage (except for Ukrainians) answering "not at all proud" (7 percent). However, asked whether they "see [themselves] as citizens of the European Union," Germans (together with Romanians) are at the top of those who "strongly disagree" (20 percent) while showing the smallest percentage of all when it comes to the "strongly agree" answer (9 percent). What these data (World Value Survey 2008) seem to suggest is a noticeable *dis*-identification of Germans with *both* their nationhood and their Europeanness.

Many experience the EU as a mixed blessing that exposes them to competition in all kinds of markets (labor, capital, goods, services) and regulates citizens' lives, while remaining cognitively, effectively and institutionally remote and inaccessible. But, given the disruptions, fears, and complaints over political and economic injustices to which the crisis and the suffering it caused in the deficit countries has given rise, the future of European integration has critically come to depend on the "subjective factor" of citizens' supportive European attitudes, preferences, and opinions and the institutional devices of consensus formation.

On the part of the losers of the banking and debt crisis, the sense of injustice being inflicted on them is twofold: being victims of *economic* decline for which they hardly can be held causally responsible *and* no longer being "masters in their own house" in terms of democratic *politics*. Both of these complaints – Europe as a liberalization machine and Europe as "foreign rule" – are, quite unsurprisingly, exacerbated by the crisis-driven and deepening divide between the surplus countries and the deficit countries within the Euro zone. Citizens of European nation states, divided as they are by the ill-considered consequences of their defective common monetary system, are under these circumstances hardly a source of energetic political agency that is needed to overcome the crisis and its different facets. What is widely shared by Europe's citizens is rather a paralyzing sense of anxiety, uncertainty, and heightened loss aversion. Yet while banks can rescue enterprises as well as other banks, states can rescue banks, the ESM and the ECB can rescue states, there is an *end* to the cascade (as the IMF will hardly step in, more than marginally and temporarily, to rescue the EU); at that end, a bootstrapping act is called for of the EU to rescue *itself* by somehow breaking the locks of the trap. But the political forces able to coax the EU to action are not in sight. They are less and less likely to come into sight as the costs of convergence, consisting in the transfer of resources that "donors" have to concede and deprivations of political autonomy that recipients must accept, are anticipated to escalate on either side of the divide. At the same time, a dissolution of the policy making capacities of the EU would not merely be, in all likelihood, irreversible; it would also put out of operation the irreplaceable tools without which the anarchy of financial markets cannot possibly be domesticated, and the devastations it has caused remedied. The tools of EU-level governance are also indispensable if encompassing, common-pool issues of public policy – energy, environment/climate, security – are to be effectively addressed in adequately far-sighted ways for which nation states cannot typically be expected to develop the ambitions nor mobilize the necessary resources.

Taken together, the above brief (yet complete, I believe) list of arguments "for" the EU and its further (democratic) integration is not sufficiently powerful in its political appeal to allow us to predict a sustained and robust alliance of popular political forces, preferences, and political parties to be inspired by any mix of them. For the EU also has its intensely and widely perceived flaws, which are highlighted and put into sharp relief by the crisis itself.

As it comes to the issues of sharing the burdens of extricating the EU from the crisis, the picture is unambiguous. "The key question is whether skeptical publics in donor countries will provide sufficient political backing to allow further bailouts."[16] A survey on

---

[16] Bechtel et al. 2014: 3.

German attitudes on this question taken in early 2012 yields telling results. Asked whether they are in favor of "bailout payments for over-indebted EU countries," 61 percent of respondents said that they are "somewhat" or "strongly" *against* such payments. Asked whether Germany should pay more or less money into the European financial rescue fund, 66 percent opt for "somewhat" or "much" *less*, while a tiny fraction of 4.5 percent is ready to pay "much" (0.5 percent) or "somewhat" (4 percent) more. These are proportions that obviously no political party aspiring for government office can afford to ignore. The analysis of the data shows that respondents are less guided by assessments of their economic interest than, near-tautologically, by their "social disposition" in favor of altruistic and cosmopolitan attitudes, which in turn are highly correlated with educational status. These favorable attitudes are seen as also deriving from "a shared sense of community and affinity" within the EU, which the authors see as "one of the most direct victims of the ongoing crisis."[17] In other words, the crisis erodes exactly those attitudes and motivations that matter as prerequisites for its solution.

The "stealth" mode of self-propelling incremental integration that neofunctionalists envisaged as an inconspicuous process engineered behind closed doors is no longer viable. To be sure, the European Union is an established condition of life for most of its citizens, something that only (though growing) minorities are opposed to on principled grounds, while majorities, also due to the multilingual nature[18] of Europe and its media,

---

[17] Ibid., 20.
[18] As of July 1, 2013, the EU has 24 official languages spoken in its 28 member states!

---

as well as due to the weakness of a European public
sphere, do not know much about, and show little interest in, what is going on in other EU countries, or at the
intransparent level of EU policy making. However, given
the disruptions, fears, and complaints over political
and economic dangers and injustices to which the crisis
has given rise, the future of European integration
has come to depend critically on the "subjective factor"
of citizens' pro-European attitudes, preferences, and
opinions.

There are two schools of thought concerning the relationship of European citizens toward their Union. One
claims that, as the EU gains authority and policy competencies, more and more citizens respond by ever
greater awareness of EU issues, get mobilized and polar-
ized – a process aptly described as "politicization."[19]
The other argues that due to the persistent democratic
deficits of the EU, (i.e., the absence of a fully developed
transnational European party system, the weakness of
the EP, the executive federalism practiced through the
Council, the lack of accountability of the unelected
Commission and the intergovernmentalism embodied in
the EC; the embryonic state of a European public sphere
bridging nation states' borders) citizens come to feel
virtually disenfranchised at the European level. That is
to say, citizens have difficulties in decoding EU politics
in terms of political "colors" that they have learned to
recognize and identify with in their national polities.
Sociologists have argued that the foundation on which
a robust integration of a society rests is the second-order
agreement on the importance of what "we" *dis*agree
about. Societies are both united and put into dynamic
motion by one core conflict, contradiction, or problem,

---

[19] Zürn and De Wilde 2012.

represented by political forces opposing each other, on the salience of which virtually everyone is in agreement. The EU polity does not have such a dominant and uniting core conflict – it has many of them with fuzzy, cross-cutting front lines, and blurred ideological divides.[20] Its citizens perceive it as an anechoic chamber where resonance of people's voices is virtually reduced to zero and the attempt to take a position structurally discouraged. They may either accept that condition fatalistically or turn to a *negative* kind of "politicization," following the logic that Peter Mair[21] has explored: Because "we cannot organize opposition *in* the EU, we are...almost forced to organize opposition *to* the EU – and become intrinsically Eurosceptic."

Euro scepticism is a cluster of attitudes and dispositions that are not easy to disentangle. There are clearly two underlying complaints. One unfolds in the "vertical" dimension of "us" *vs* "Brussels," with the complaint being that too many policy matters have been taken out of the arena of national politics and shifted to a European level where accountability mechanisms are weak. The other is "horizontal" and relates to the conflict between the two sides of the new European divide. In both cases, there is a mix of complaints over *political* and *economic* injustices. The former has to do with a strong sense of deprivation and disenfranchisement, amounting to a sense of having become subject

---

[20] It seems plainly inconceivable that political personalities as different in their political convictions as Olli Rehn, a committed market liberal, and László Andor, an equally committed Leftist social policy innovator, could ever coexist as cabinet members of any national government. Yet both of them are EU commissioners.
[21] Mair 2007: 7.

---

to a kind of foreign rule. In contrast, economic injustice is emphasized when those who have in no way caused the crisis are made to pay for it, while the banks who have played a causal role get bailed out at taxpayers' expense. The latter distributional complaint can then be elaborated, referring to some "moral hazard" intuition, in a Leftist "class *vs* class" reading and a rightist "country *vs* country" reading. Either of these readings has become a fertile seedbed for conflicting populist movements.

7

The Configuration of Political Forces and Preferences

Jürgen Habermas has pointed at the two main dimensions in which differences of political forces (be they individuals, political parties and their alliances, national governments, political intellectuals, etc.) on issues of European integration can be represented.[1] These are the dimension of (a) national *vs* (b) supranational preferences and (1) left-of-center preferences favoring market-constraining forms of governance and "positive" integration *vs* (2) right-of-center preferences for market-making strategies and negative integration. A simple cross-tabulation of these dichotomized dimensions yields the following typology:

	National (a)	Supranational (b)
Left (1)	Renationalization of class conflict	Positive integration of "social Europe"
Right (2)	Rightist anti-integration populism	Neoliberal negative integration

---

[1] Habermas 2013b: 83.

Let me start in the South East with b2, the *market-making pro-integrationist* position. European integration is welcomed for several of its alleged advantages. First, European-wide markets based upon the four freedoms offer opportunities for reaping economies of scale and for launching capital-intensive transnational cooperation projects in sectors such as defense and aerospace industries, energy, communication, and R&D in other advanced technologies. Second, the funding and regulation of such projects will be taken out of national political arenas. Thirdly and most importantly, national institutional systems (ranging from pensions to public radio and TV to state-owned banks to status rights of trade unions) will be uprooted under the combined impact of economic rivalry between states (exploited by investors for "regime shopping" and tax avoidance purposes) and judicial action of the ECJ eliminating "rigidities" and obstacles to access of potential competitors to investment opportunities and product markets. Also, market integration activates tax competition among member states trying to attract investors, with the effect of slimming down "wasteful" public expenditures and steadily bringing down rates of corporate taxation. In sum, neoliberal protagonists of European market integration with uniform regulation, welcome advances of the European project because they see it as a normatively undemanding and depoliticized force of competitiveness-enhancing economic modernization. In a Europe-wide market without a Europe-wide democratic polity, "market justice" trumps "social justice", as Streeck[2] has argued. For practitioners of neoliberalism, the EU's "democratic deficit" is a virtue rather than a vice, as it helps to fend off political

---

[2] Streeck 2014.

interferences into the dynamics of the transnational markets as constituted by the four freedoms. The emphasis here is on *production*, entrepreneurship, factor mobility to optimize allocation and bring down labor costs, increasing efficiency and the maximal integration of human resources in productive processes – not on *(re) distribution*. A virtual ban on issues of distribution and, in particular, inter-state redistribution (such as debt mutualization or Euro bonds) is institutionalized by intergovernmentalism and the unanimity governing decision making at the level of the EC. At the level of member states and regarding intra-state redistribution, this ban is achieved by the principle of "subsidiarity" relegating social policy to member state policy making unless, that is, policy is seen to distort competition or/ and to cause impermissible budget deficits. As to the competition of entire member state economies, the political leaders of those states that are performing better than others in terms of trade surpluses can claim evolutionary superiority for their institutions and policies and demand, as a condition of assistance, that relative losers reform themselves by emulating the winners' example.

(b1) The *market-constraining pro-integrationist* political perspective envisions an EU that emulates the accomplishments of post-war democratic welfare states at the supranational level. Seen from this left-of-center perspective, the EU is – or should credibly be transformed into – "Social Europe,"[3] a political entity that is not just the scene of unfettered competition and factor mobility but at the same time protects the victims of market competition and enables them to cope with its challenges. Any economic competition produces winners (including indirect winners benefiting from supposedly

---

[3] Cf. the digital periodical Social Europe Journal.

better or cheaper products emerging victorious from competition). Yet it also produces *losers*. Some of the losers can adjust and make a new start in the next round of the game. Others cannot and fall victim to poverty, unemployment and precariousness. The capacity of losers to adjust and stay in the competitive game at acceptable conditions (as defined by social rights) is contingent upon public provision of transfers and services, the latter must be *mandated and guaranteed* at the EU level and "social Europe," rather than being allowed to be eroded in the competition of investors, workers, and member states. As any serious guarantee of social rights and "social inclusion" must involve substantial *redistribution* (between regions, social classes, economic sectors, generations, member states, points in time) of material resources, a *democratic* polity is needed in which the European citizenry is represented, conflicting distributional claims are processed, and taxing and spending rights vested. Without a vigorous policy of redistribution, including international redistribution, anything resembling socio-economic "convergence" is unlikely to occur. Without convergence, however, the economic legitimation of the European Union having created a "level playing field" is a plain sham. It is only if such convergence, or a European guarantee of social rights and economic protection is perceived to be a credible ambition of integration that the European "project" will win back some of the support of its EU citizens it has so clearly lost. The reason why the guarantee of tolerable competitive outcomes can no longer be redeemed at the level of *national* welfare states (and in the name of "subsidiarity") is easy to see: Member states have themselves become actors in the competitive game; integration has turned them into "competition states" which typically have responded to competitive challenges by economizing on taxes and social expenses. Hence welfare states will either be firmly re-anchored at the level of a constitutionally consolidated supranational European polity or their component parts will float like driftwood, driven by the currents of border-crossing market competition. Yet any attempt "to rescue the *Sozialer Rechtsstaat* [the German concept referring to a welfare state that is based on constitutional rights] at the supranational level"[4] is doomed to fail as long as the intergovernmental procedure of the EC, its unanimity rule, endows each of its members, deficit and surplus states alike, with a *liberum veto*.

(a2) *Rightist anti-integration populism.* Defending the national interest and identity by seeking social shelter and economic protection from integration behind national borders: *the anti-European political Right*. As the political Left is torn between its cultural libertarianism and its *étatiste* concept of a desirable social order, the political Right is even more deeply disunited between its economic libertarianism (summarized above, as it applies to European integration) and its cultural and political ethno-nationalism. The latter is the main characteristic of Rightist anti-integration political forces. For them, the key reference point is the national political community, which, as an eternal community of fate, must be protected, in cultural as well as socio-economic terms (and, if need be, by military force) by a strong national leadership in government. The complaints that proponents of this perspective have with the EU are twofold. First, the EU is denounced as a supranational agency that illegitimately imposes its rules and conditions, including those relating to the common currency, upon "us," the nation. This "vertical" front of conflict with "Brussels"

---

[4] Fossum and Menéndez 2011: 224.

---

is exacerbated by a second, horizontal, front dividing member state nations: Europe allows "them" (e.g. migrants from the south east of the EU and on the basis of the full EU mobility rights, fully effective since January 2014) to benefit from "our" resources; and Europe allows "them" (e.g. German representatives in the EC or the Council) to impose their rules and conditions upon "us" or deny us the resources "we" depend upon. Taken together, these two confrontational frames add up to viewing the EU as an agency of foreign rule against which the nation must defend itself. What must our leaders defend us against by strengthening borders, asserting identity, and reclaiming sovereignty? Answers range from foreign goods and investors to foreign people to "foreign gods." Anti-European mobilization from the nationalist Right is often amalgamated with anti-liberal, anti-democratic, semi-authoritarian and religious political doctrines and affects. Paradoxically enough, it is the occasion of the EP elections of 2014 that has provided the anti-European Right with the opportunity to mobilize and to form transnational alliances that are predicted to win up to one third of EP seats.

Populist anti-European mobilization[5] is to be found on both sides of the new European divide. Northern Rightist "populists" (as well as centrist political parties fearing the success of populist competitors) reject further tax-funded transfers and credit guarantees, while their Southern Leftist analogues reject measures being imposed upon them that they denounce as being part of a victimization of their nation in which their political elites are willing accomplices. Both profit from the crisis

---

[5] Leonard and Torreblanca (2013) offer a fine-grained typology of European populist parties and different brands of Euroscepticism.

by widening their political support. In all cases, they are engaged in pure *"politics,"* successfully scandalizing the EU and the Euro by appealing to resentments, fears, and national identities, yet have little or nothing to offer in terms of *"policy,"* as it comes to designing and proposing remotely feasible and effective strategies out of the crisis.

(a1) *Renationalization of class conflict.* A fundamental Leftist critique of European integration (as opposed to a critique of specific EU policies, from arms exports to the liberalization of health services) is a relatively novel phenomenon. While Leftist populists (e.g. in Greece, Spain and Italy) have successfully mobilized by blaming the EU for causing (or mismanaging) the debt crisis and the associated economic and social crisis, a clear theoretical statement of a Leftist integration critique has recently been pioneered by Wolfgang Streeck.[6] Streeck demonstrates that the common currency has not just divided the members of the Euro zone but also led to their political expropriation. According to him, plans for further economic and political integration of European nations amount to a coercive homogenization that is economically hopeless and politically undesirable. He offers a non-nationalist normative argument for the renationalization of economic and monetary policies in Europe, one that can be tuned to the specific needs and conditions of member states and their populations. According to him, the nation state and its democratic political institutions which used to serve as the foremost arena of class conflict must be re-conquered as a bastion of resistance, at the elite and, in particular, at the mass level, against the "neoliberal-supranational Leviathan" of finance capitalism as it reigns the EU. In a

---

[6] Streeck 2013; Streeck 2014.

controversy with Jürgen Habermas,[7] the latter criticized him for his "defeatist forsaking of the European project." Apart from this normative controversy, the further elaboration of Streeck's radical critique seems to be in need of defending itself to three challenges. First, it is hard to see with whom, even in the European periphery of Euro losers, a Leftist renationalization project is (or might become) even minimally popular; so much for realism. Second, the project would imply that the victims of the neoliberal regime release the regime's proponents and beneficiaries from the responsibility to compensate the losers, or at least assist them in their recovery; if victims leave the arena of EU politics, they basically eliminate their chances of obtaining any assistance or compensation to which they can lay very legitimate claims. Third, the narrative of the Euro regime as a definitive and irreversible victory of neoliberal political forces remains contested. As long as it is contested, a "forward-looking" alternative cannot be easily dismissed – the alternative perspective that it is only a democratically renovated system of European economic, fiscal and social policy making, everything that can be subsumed under my b2 type – that can cope with the crisis. As we know from Hirschman:[8] You can still exit once your voice has fallen on deaf ears; you can threaten exit as long as you are in; yet your voice becomes useless *after* you have in fact exited as there is no one left to talk to or willing to listen. After exiting the Europe-wide arena of potential policy reversals and constitutional advances, the scope and degree of inclusiveness of crisis responses would be rendered hopelessly smaller compared with the scope of (inter)dependencies in

---

[7] Habermas 2013a.
[8] Hirschman 1970.

---

which the crisis is rooted. What would prevail after renationalization of policies is the dynamics of spontaneous mutual adjustment of national polities, policies, and economies doing without the capacity of a supranational regime. The capacity for control would even decrease, by orders of magnitude, compared to the present and highly deficient governing capacity of the Commission and other EU institutions. The spontaneity of conflicting national actors is hardly something that thoughtful proponents of the a1 political perspective would seriously consider banking on.

It is not my ambition here to assess the relative strength of the four perspectives my typology may help to recognize and distinguish. These perspectives unfold in interaction with one another, with a1, a2, and b1 all being adopted and advocated in opposition and as a corrective to the hegemonic force of b2. Two of them (a1 and a2) focus on confrontational *politics* with strong appeals to (or a hypothetical role for) political action from below with its emotional ingredients of fear, anger, and contempt, while the other two (b1 and b2) describe encompassing elite perspectives for the design of EU *policies*. One pair (a1 and b1) belongs to the political Left and the other (a2 and b2) to the political Right, although it is hard to imagine that these two factions within their respective political camp could easily agree on common strategies. The overall picture indicates that political dispositions for action concerning the Euro zone and the further course of European integration are highly fragmented and deeply divided along the left/right, national/supranational and creditor/debtor country axes. The result is a pervasive paralysis of agency.[9]

---

[9] Tsoukalis (2014: 62) rightly speaks of an "unstable equilibrium" that is "prone to accidents".

8

Germany's Leadership Role for Europe: A Non-Starter

One putative way out of this scarcity of vigorous and consistent political agency is that Germany adopts the role of political leadership in Europe, as various voices[1] have demanded (or even stated as a matter of fact), from inside, and even more often outside the country.

As in the tango, it takes *two* to exercise leadership. Whether or not Germany is *ready* to shoulder that role is the less serious of two questions. Given the volume of distributional challenges and political responsibilities involved, the answer to this question is a resounding "no." Otmar Issing, the ECB's former chief economist, leading member of the von Hayek society and Germany's authoritative proponent of policy perspectives guiding the Merkel government, provides a clear and concise version of all the standard *topoi*.[2] "The argument for German leadership boils down," he warns, "to a plea that it should put more...money on the European table." From the official German point of

---

[1] Schmitz and Soros 2014; Bolaffi 2013.
[2] The following quotes from Issing 2014.

---

view, such imposition must of course be resisted. After all, why should one country's taxpayers be liable "for the irresponsible practices of another country's banks?," he asks. In the official German discourse, this interest argument is unfailingly backed up (not to say: camouflaged) by a decency argument: "*Deutschland* as *Führer* – this slogan has something of a frightening ring." Germany refuses to lead actively, but if others are ready to be "led by [German] example," they are welcome to do so to their (most likely) benefit. One thing, however, must be clear: Germany is not going to "reward bad policies" by giving its consent to Eurobonds or other forms of debt mutualization, as "each country is responsible for its own policies... The countries now in trouble have caused their own problems through their own policy mistakes."

This quasi-official discourse exhibits two characteristics: it is entirely "upstream" and methodologically "nationalist." That is to say, policies are being advocated in terms of what or who (allegedly) *caused* the problem, not in terms of downstream *consequences* and solutions. And the discourse presupposes that the causes of one country's malaise must exclusively be looked for *within* that country and the flawed action of its political elites, not in the flawed design of the Euro and/or external shocks. Rather than taking an explicit strategic position on the future of the Euro zone as a whole, the official discourse of Germany pleads for its own inaction and otherwise lectures others about "sound economics." It apparently does not register with champions of this discourse that letting others suffer from the consequences of their allegedly own "bad policies" may itself turn out to be bad policy in terms of the long-term interests of everyone else, including self-satisfied bystanders and advocates of "sound" policies.

What Issing offers here is a crude case of "methodological nationalism," also known as "flower pot theory." In essence it suggests that whatever happens in and to a nation must be accounted for in terms of what has happened inside that nation (its history, national character etc.) conceived of as an isolated container. This framing strategy involves two fallacies. One is a fallacy of composition: whatever the consequences of "bad policies" may be, they do not affect "the nation" as a whole but specific classes, regions, generations and other social categories within the national society in highly unequal ways. Not "Greece" is suffering from those consequences, but Greek patients, unemployed, civil servants, etc. while other segments of Greek society remain entirely unaffected. The other is a fallacy involved in the mental practice of "national" framing that is one of decomposition: It ascribes events and developments that result from the transnational interaction and interdependency of forces inside the "container", thereby de-emphasizing explanatory factors originating from beyond national borders such as interventions by the "Troika."

Be that as it may. Even if German political elites were ready explicitly and formally to *accept* a hegemonic role (instead of just using the de facto *power* of "Madame No" to set conditions behind closed doors while denying any leadership responsibility), the second question is whether Germany would be *granted any authority to lead* by those who would then have to comply with its leadership. Again, the answer is no. Even if we disregard the historical precedent, rooted in the collective memory of many European nations, of Germany trying to establish itself through military aggression as the ruler of the continent during the Second World War, much more recent memories of the widely resented role the German Bundesbank has played prior to the Euro (as well as the role the German government has played during the crisis) clearly hinder Germany from being appointed by fellow-Europeans as their benevolent hegemon, entrusted with the mission to lead Europe out of the crisis. The awareness that they *depend*, for better or worse, on external effects of German economic policies does not logically imply the desire to *comply* with policies made by German governments. It is not just that Germany and its grand coalition political elites are unwilling to lead Europe out of the crisis; it is also highly unlikely that others would chose to be led by Germany. For both of these reasons, the proposal[3] to assign Germany that leadership role (or to assign it to a Franco-German tandem) must be considered an outright non-starter. If this is so, we need to make the leadership role of Germany or any other member state dispensable. That could only be accomplished if a *supra*-national mechanism of crisis resolution and economic, fiscal, and social policy making were put in place, one that is endowed with legitimacy by all European citizens, not just by the voters of one or two large member states.

The discourses and narratives surrounding the crisis are markedly different from member state to member state and frame both politics and policies. "Framing" is a rhetorical practice by which speakers do not *describe* an object but *add meaning* to a description by putting it in perspective, shaping expectations, evaluating it, drawing pragmatic lessons, and setting an agenda as to how to deal with it. Whether we say that a glass is half full or half empty is not a matter of controversy over facts (there can be none), but an implicit and unspoken suggestion of how to "read" the phenomenon in question and what standards and expectations to apply

---

[3] Bolaffi 2013.

---

when dealing with it. Similarly the frame of a painting does two things: It emphasizes and decorates what is worth looking at, and it limits and conceals from our view what supposedly is not worth being seen and deservedly relegated to the invisible. Frames are thus positively and negatively selective social constructs that can be strategically chosen in order to make others adopt a perspective suggested by the framer. They can also derive from given ambiguities inherent in the language used and can be strategically exploited by political actors and media communicators.

The latter is the case with two striking equivocations peculiar to the German language that have played a role in the framing of the crisis in Germany (and Austria) and in shaping the domestic support for policies. These equivocations come with the terms *Haushalt* (referring both to an established economic entity of private consumption, such as a family household with its furniture, equipment, and financial assets *and* a budget of state authorities) and the term *Schuld* (referring both to guilt feelings and the attribution of negative sanctions as a consequence of someone's moral or legal wrongdoing *and* the status and obligations of being a debtor – *Schuldner*). Let me outline briefly the policy implications that follow from the strategic use of these two semantic ambiguities and the misguided analogies they suggest.

First, if a state *budget* is likened to a family *household*, a number of differences between the two are deemphasized and normative prescriptions associated with one of the two claimed as applying to the other as well. Chancellor Merkel made herself (in)famous by stating at a convention of her party, held a few weeks after the meltdown of the Lehman bank on 9/15, 2008 in Stuttgart/ Swabia, that "as the Swabian housewife knows," nobody can live beyond his means forever. This seemingly trivial proposition was successfully designed to establish the moral truth of austerity policy. It is rich in its connotations: The reference to Swabia, the most prosperous region of Germany and famous for its industrious work ethic, serves to allude to the economic pay-off of virtue. The inhabitants of Swabia are widely stereotyped as being thrifty, frugal, hard-working, and entrepreneurial. The figure of the housewife represents the guardian of family virtue who is in charge of *spending* the family income (as opposed to the male head of the household who supposedly *earns* it). Her simple-minded yet iron principle is not to overspend the income and save for hard times or, proverbially, for building a house for the family. What must be avoided, for the sake of the family's honor, is two things: to become dependent upon others through incurring debt and to make the children pay for debt they have inherited from their parents. Speaking as a leading politician (and a woman endorsing the point of view of the housewife), the speaker suggests that this moral wisdom should also directly apply to fiscal and budgetary policy one-to-one.

This analogy is equally powerful and deceptive.[4] It is deceptive due to its implicit denial, facilitated by the two meanings of the single word *Haushalt*, of the *differences* between the economic conduct of an individual family household and a state budget. For one thing, a family household is, in economic terms, a private matter with a beginning in time and an end, while a state budget is an element in a presumably endless chain of iterated annual political decision making performed by some elected legislative body concerning the state's revenues and expenditures. Secondly, the supposed immorality of

---

[4] European Trade Union Institute 2013: 8.

making your children pay for the debt you leave behind does not apply to the state budget and its reliance on sovereign debt because the often invoked "future generation" by necessity consists not just of *debtors* but also of *creditors* who have inherited claims against their contemporary debtors; this fact may well lead to issues of redistribution among members, i.e., debtors *and* the heirs of creditors, of that future generation, issues which will have to be left to them to settle among themselves by political means. Thirdly, the moralizing tale of the Swabian housewife is based upon a fallacy of composition: What may be right for any *one* of us cannot possibly be right for *all* of us: Not everyone can be a net saver (or, for that matter, exporter), as the resulting demand gap would amount to a veritable prescription for severe and cumulative recession. Some *must* live, in a capitalist market society, *beyond* their (presently available) means, e.g. investors who buy credit in order to engage in entrepreneurial operations the profitability of which (and hence the potential to redeem the debt) is never an *ex ante* certainty.

Nevertheless, the housewife frame of budgetary policy remains powerful because it serves as a blinder against the three dis-analogies just mentioned and hence as an excuse to eliminate them from political consideration. That effect is exacerbated by the second equivocation of *Schuld* (guilt) and *Schuldner* (debtor). As the Swabian housewife is the embodiment of economic virtue and wisdom, the guilty debtor personifies the morally deficient. The equations that follow are obvious: The debtor is morally inferior – guilty – because he lacks the self-control necessary to live within the limits of his means; that is to say: *not* because his low income and poor social security forces him to rely on consumer credit, *not* because uniquely cheap credit, facilitated by faulty monetary policy, plus lax conditions have offered him an irresistible opportunity to purchase "subprime" mortgages, *not* because actors in the financial industry were granting credit frivolously because they could confidently expect to be bailed out according to the "too-big-to-fail" logic in case something "goes wrong," and *not* because sovereign debtors have incurred debt in order to stimulate investment and employment in the "real" economy – all these possibilities are being obscured and excluded from consideration through the "guilt" frame. Because of the deeply engrained moral inferiority of the debtor, any debt relief (or, in the Euro context, debt mutualization through Euro bonds etc.) would be an unwise, positively counter-productive move as it would lead the debtor to engage in "moral hazard" behavior, thus further exploiting the provider of relief instead of "reforming" himself according to the self-sufficiency command of economic virtue. Note that this logic of moralizing victim blaming, at least in its crudest and most popular version, invites an amalgamation of the *good vs evil* with the *us vs them* code of *national* collectivities as moral agents.[5] It is the combination of these two codes and their underlying frames that shapes much of the current discourse on the monetary and fiscal future of the Euro zone and the EU as a whole. This discourse, I submit, operates as a mechanism that helps to keep the trap locked.

This short application of framing theory in the context of some peculiar ambiguities of the German language is of course not to claim that the crisis (and the situation of being "trapped" in it) can be accounted for in

---

[5] In Germany, it has been a routine practice of even such quality papers as *Süddeutsche Zeitung* to refer summarily to the PIIGS countries as "fiscal sinners."

terms of politically constructed frames alone. It is just intended to show how linguistic ambiguities can be exploited, in Germany and Austria (and in Dutch as well),[6] for political purposes that in other countries must be achieved by more explicitly ideological claims.

On November 28, 2011, on the occasion of an official visit to Berlin, the Polish foreign minister Radek Sikorski addressed an audience, pointing out that Germany is the biggest beneficiary of the Euro and has "the biggest obligation to make [it] sustainable." Here we have an equivocation of "interest" and "obligation": the speaker tries to deduce an "obligation" from the fact that the actor in question reaps a benefit. He pleads that his host may recognize and fulfill the alleged obligation: "The biggest threat to the security and prosperity of Europe would be the collapse of the Euro zone...I fear German power less than I am beginning to fear German inactivity." "You have become Europe's indispensable nation... You may not fail to lead. Not dominate, but to lead to reform."

No doubt the minister is right about the benefits: Financial investors have been fleeing from investments in risky bonds of the deficit countries, seeking the safe haven of German bonds. As a consequence, German real borrowing costs have been lower (in fact negative) than they would be in "normal" times. Also, Germany profits from favorable external value of the Euro, which allows it to remain Europe's export champion. Saving "Greece" and "Ireland" has to a large extent been an indirect way of saving investments "systemic" German banks had made in those countries. There is also a long-term interest in keeping clients of German exports able to import, which they would be largely unable to do

---

[6] Mak 2012: 100.

once they had to leave the Euro zone. There is also a *negative* political interest of Germany, an interest in something that must be avoided: the interest in not having "to take the blame for an economic or political disaster close to home."[7] But all of these *interests* of its own do not add up to an "obligation," a claim recognized as *legitimately* made by specific others and therefore as binding.

Political obligations of this kind are those of *solidarity*.[8] They are more limited than moral duties (which apply to the interaction with *all* human beings) and more extensive than legal duties (which are established by positive law enforced through state power). They also differ from the obligations applying to the members of a "given" community, such as a family. What norms of solidarity apply to is the universe of members of an *intended* community, seen as a project under construction. This conforms to the historical origin of the concept of solidarity with its roots in the French revolution (building a republic) and the working-class movements (aiming at some realization of freedom and justice, sometimes called "socialism"). As I have tried to show, in the case of the EU a vision of a shared and normatively substantiated "project" has largely faded away and, with it, the disposition to comply with duties the fulfillment of which is thought to be beneficial to "all of us" (with the scope of "us" still being under expansive redefinition). What remains as a source of obligations are intuitions concerning fairness: If one and the same institutional arrangement (say, the Euro) has turned out to operate to the advantage of some members of a legally constituted

---

[7] Tsoulakis 2014: 60.
[8] Cf. the discussion of the concept of solidarity in Habermas (2013b: 100–11).

---

community (of all EU citizens) while inflicting serious disadvantages and suffering on others, then the latter should be assisted by the former. If the lucky "winners" fail to comply with this obligation, they can and should be denounced as free-riders who (selfishly and possibly unwisely) violate norms of fairness against others with whom they share a legal community. Within this framework of a relatively undemanding elaboration of what "solidarity" might mean in the context of the current crisis, much remains to be specified by political processes. These determine what demands the losers make, how sensitive the winners to these demands, and to what extent and to whom assistance is actually delivered.

Yet the German coalition government inaugurated in late 2013 wavered; Germany pursues its interests but defies what Sikorski calls its "obligations." It dominates (by insisting on the unilateral right to decide on the terms of trade between "solidarity" and "consolidation") but does not lead. It stands in the way of the building of an enhanced *European* (Euro zone) governing capacity endowed with a *supranational* leadership role – the only thing that could make *German* leadership dispensable. Germany dominates by refusal to share its resources across national borders as well as across the divides of social classes according to standards of fairness as opposed to a calculus of interest and discipline. Its reluctance to assume a leadership position may be well founded: If Sikorski does not fear German power (or, rather, fears it "less"), his point of view may not be widely shared in the deficit countries who have come to frame their disastrous current social and economic conditions as a result of Germany's intransigence to concede measures of debt mutualization and its insistence on austerity and "reform" measures. Equally rightly, German political elites feel that a German assumption of leadership role would be a (costly) project, given these perceptions and memories of others, which would not be endorsed by national constituencies within the country. Therefore, Sikorski might address the wrong actor (as does Bolaffi with his passionate call for German "leadership"). Or, more precisely, addresses the actor with the wrong demand. The "right" demand would be to call upon Germany not to "lead," but to surrender some of its power and economic resources in favor of capabilities for *European* instead of German leadership – that is to say, to let the "indispensable" nation make itself dispensable as a leader.

Yet it is exactly that demand that German political elites, fearing adverse reactions from their constituencies, are so far unwilling even to consider. But constituencies and their preferences are never "given"; they can be informed and enlightened by political leaders who are willing and capable of encouraging voters to find out what they "really" want, or come to recognize they should want. It remains to be seen to what extent (if any) the new German grand coalition government, based as it is upon a coalition compact emphasizing the principle of "budgetary sovereignty"[9] (a euphemism for saying "don't expect any assistance from us!") for all Euro member states, will change this hesitancy to take constructive steps toward EU-level institution-building. Timid elites prefer to ban the consideration of such steps from public discourse.

---

[9] The key sentence is: "The principle that each member state is responsible for its liabilities must be preserved. Any kind of debt mutualization would jeopardize the necessary orientation of national policies. National budgetary responsibility and supranational liability for debt are incompatible." (my translation, C. O.)

The practice of German-promoted austerity conditionalism has so far been an exercise in the government's power to say "no" without the readiness to assume responsibility, that is, to say "yes" to any way out of the disastrous social and economic implications of that "no." Negative externalities inflicted by German intransigence upon other participants in the Euro game are met, in the name of a more and more fictitious "sovereignty," with positively institutionalized blindness. Instead, near-lethal doses of "financial discipline" and "structural reform" are being administered to the deficit countries as prescriptions for medium-term recovery, while the short-term management of the crisis is left to the Troika regime and the ECB's legally dubious practice of throwing unlimited amounts of money at problems that result from *institutional* defects of the EMU. While such tactics may help to foreclose "debate on questions that are politically difficult in Germany, such as the introduction of jointly guaranteed Eurozone bonds,"[10] the question remains whether the wait-and-see attitude, occasionally papered-over with last-minute concessions and gestures of empathy to the plight of the Euro losers, will do anything to cope with the ongoing banking, budget, economic, social, and, above all, institutional crisis of the EU. Yet it is arguably not in the best German long-term interest to pursue nothing *but* its short-term interest. As the senior German student of the political economy of European integration has compellingly observed, "social catastrophes and political explosions can only be avoided through massive transfers from the more prosperous parts of the Monetary Union."[11] There is no serious evidence showing that that conclusion is

---

[10] Peel 2012.
[11] Scharpf 2014: 176.

---

questionable. There is just the virtually uniform if opportunistic reluctance of political elites to say so in public.

On the other hand, there is no calculus available that would let actors in the core know how much they will have to pay in order to serve their long-term interests. Regrettably, history is not a market. You cannot ever be certain about whether gains realized will be worth the sacrifices made. If you fail to commit yourself to principles of solidarity and European-wide cosmopolitanism and overcome your obsession with suspecting others of playing moral hazard games against you, chances are that you end up violating even your most selfish interests. After all, in case one or more of the deficit member states were to default on the loans they have received from the ESM and declare insolvency, one or more of the surplus countries would have to foot the bill of that default, with roughly a quarter of the loss falling on Germany alone.[12] Both the disruption of the Euro monetary system and/or the stigmatization of core countries as causing through inaction catastrophic conditions in the periphery would clearly amount to a violation of those most selfish interests.

On both sides of the new core-periphery divide, we find characteristic discursive maneuvers of building political arguments. Without having the space here to explore the sociology of knowledge of the Euro and debt crisis in any further detail, I just wish to suggest four generalizations concerning the mental tactics by which elites typically address their constituencies and each other. First, speakers for the core, as we have seen in the case of Mr Issing, tend to use "upstream," or deontic, constructs while those in the periphery address

---

[12] Schmitz and Soros 2014: 91.

their problems in a "downstream," or consequentialist, perspective. The former perspective helps to establish the normative argument following the logic of *pacta sunt servanda*, blaming others for having broken contracts or having committed policy mistakes for which they must now, in line with the Treaties, accept liability. The downstream perspective, in contrast, emphasizes adverse consequences of the crisis that will obtain as grim counterfactuals in case the assistance they call for is not granted: nobody can be expected to comply with a suicide pact that he has mistakenly entered into, no matter whose mistake, error, or false promise it was.

Secondly, speakers of the core tend to frame their diagnosis in terms of deliberate political wrongdoing of nations and their political leaders, while their counterparts in the periphery cite international contexts (such as the US subprime crisis) or their being victims of mistaken information and advice as causal in order to exculpate themselves and former ruling elites of respective countries. Third, core speakers insist that assistance and transfers requested by periphery actors are *costs*, expenses of national governments, acting as fiduciary actors managing national wealth, that are legitimately subject to rational calculation and *economizing moves*: the less "we" have to pay the better. Their counterparts in the south, in contrast, portray these very same expenses as being mandated by *solidaristic obligations* and commitments, which prospective donors must fulfill *without* calculating their economic worthiness as investments. Finally, both sides defend their perspective by a subsidiary argument pointing out that what is "good for *us*" will in time turn out, in the end and with the proviso of "self interest, rightly understood," "good for *you*" as well. In this manner, even the core's harshest and most selfish conditionalist demand for "reforms" can be

advertised as bitter yet necessary medicine of modernization," while the periphery can hint at a scenario
according to which practicing solidarity is in fact in the
long-term political and economic interest of those who
do so; after all, the recovery of the periphery will also
stabilize export markets of the core countries, while its
further social and economic decay will cost the core
dearly.

None of these rhetorical moves and propositions are
"true" in any compelling way. All they can be is "per-
suasive" to constituencies and counterparts on the other
side of the divide. Yet that persuasiveness is itself contingent upon the extent to which European integration
is considered a shared project rooted in a common
political identity and citizenship. My sketch of a balance
sheet of net motivations supporting further European
integration suggests that this confident sense of Europe
being a project from the realization of which "all of us"
will eventually benefit is wearing thin under the impact
of the crisis itself.

Not even the "upstream" paradigm of concentrating
on the causes of the crisis and attaching blame according to "wrong policies" yields robust diagnoses. If
someone has submitted fraudulent reports on Greek
sovereign debt, were there perhaps others who willingly
allowed themselves to be deceived? Was perhaps the
assumption, built into the Maastricht treaty, that deficit
criteria could at all be enforced through sanctions, a
maneuver of wishful self-deception with which its pro-
moters cannot expect to get away undamaged? If the
Spanish government set up incentives, which then
inflated the construction bubble in that country, could
they really have known better? Germany, France as well
as everyone else were warned about the flawed currency
zone and the poor policy capacities associated with the

common currency; why were these warnings not heeded? Before engaging in nation *vs* nation blame games, it may be advisable to let future historians do their job. They may well come up with the finding that a mix of ignorance (of both the forgivable and unforgivable kind), irresponsibility and the pursuit of ill-conceived interests were at the root of the crisis to which essentially "all of us" have contributed through action and inaction and in abeyance of the mode of operation of financial capitalism.

In the meantime, let us take to heart one analytical distinction concerning answers to the question "Who is responsible?" The distinction is between "causal responsibility" and "remedial responsibility."[13] The distinction is simple but has weighty implications. Causal responsibility concerns what you *have* done, remedial responsibility what you *can* (afford to) do. The latter implies that the *less* an agent (member state and its economy) has suffered as a consequence of the mistakes made collectively or the *more* it even has benefited from them having been made, the *greater* the share of the burdens the agent must shoulder in compensating others for adverse consequences resulting from the original mistake. This moral calculus can even converge with mandates of prudence, suggesting that the national entity least negatively affected will have a long-term interest in preserving an arrangement that has yielded it so many benefits at comparatively low costs. Whatever the mix of obligation and interest, the answer to the question of who the entity might be that bears the greatest remedial responsibility in today's Europe is compelling: it is Germany. Yet German political elites and publics refuse to appreciate this answer as compelling

---

[13] Cf. Offe 2013.

and to act accordingly. This is unsurprising. Why, after all, should we expect that those who are affected least by the crisis (and even benefited from it) be inclined to make it a priority to remedy it? To do so would require that German political elites not only commit themselves (and their constituencies!) to a normative vision of European integration that has largely evaporated, as I have argued, under the impact of the crisis. Failing this normative commitment, there still remains a strong argument from prudential reasoning for Germany doing "whatever it takes" to rescue the common currency from its decay. This argument consists of two parts, referring to the opportunity costs and the direct costs resulting from the currency zone's disintegration. First, Germany "is the greatest beneficiary of a stable Euro zone and thus has to fear most from its disintegration."[14] Second, the letter of the "Treaty Establishing the European Stability Mechanism" of 2012, endorsed by the German Constitutional Court, states in its article 9, 3 that "ESM Members hereby irrevocably and unconditionally undertake to pay on demand any capital call made on them...; such demand [is] to be paid within seven days of receipt." Given that the direct costs applying to Germany amount to more than a quarter of any such call, any German government has strong incentives indeed to prevent conditions under which such demand were to materialize in response to an emergency encountered by a Euro zone member.

Yet in spite of these weighty prudential considerations, an amazingly relaxed approach is reflected in the coalition treaty concluded as the basis of government policy between Christian Democrats and Social Democrats in December 2013. "Many Germans," comments

---

[14] Schmitz and Soros 2014: 25.

a senior German diplomat and policy analyst "feel happy with the status quo. They see no necessity for all-too-ambitious steps to expand the EU, or proposals for reform, have no interest in great strategic questions and would prefer to be left in peace."[15] So much for "German leadership." And leading economic policy expert Marcel Fratzscher observes a "policy of small steps, reactive rather than proactive"; in his view, the German government is "remarkably noncommittal on Europe."[16]

---

[15] *New York Times*, December 16, 2013.
[16] Ibid.

9
"Thin" Citizenship: The Ugly Face of the EU System of Rule

The regime type by which the European Union is governed is a peculiar kind of non-state. It provides for a "thin" and highly mediated kind of citizenship that yields, as Peter Mair's quote above suggests, very limited opportunities of its practice. The EU regime has a supreme judicial power, the ECJ, and a supreme monetary power, the ECB – both of which are out of reach of any formal political accountability, as is the Commission, which initiates legislation and is headed by a president who is nominated by the EC and elected by the EP. Article 17 TEU stipulates that the Commission shall "promote the general interest of the Union" without bothering to take note of the fact that the meaning of that "general interest" is essentially controversial among political parties and other collective actors and can only be concretized as an outcome of political contestation – which, however, is not allowed to take place as the Commissioners' "independence [presumably from political parties? CO] must be beyond doubt" (ibid.). The members of the EC are of course elected, if not *with the mission* of ruling *Europe* but as political leaders of their *national* polities. The same applies to the Council. Only the members of the EP are elected by *European* citizens (if according to *national* election laws of member states) for the purpose of ruling Europe through legislation, although the EP shares its law-making competencies with the Council.

The supreme policy making body and gate keeper of the EU is the non-partisan intergovernmental (as opposed to supranational) European Council. It consists of the heads of state or heads of government of member states; "Europe," as it were, does not have a seat at the table.[1] It meets at least four times per year and defines the directions and priorities of the EU and gives "impulses" for EU policies; it is not involved in European law-making. (After its sessions, almost always in Brussels, a subtotal of the members, those belonging to the Euro zone, stay on for separate consultations.) The mode of decision making of this body (that meets behind closed doors) is peculiar: no votes are taken, but the president of the Council draws a "conclusion" which is considered adopted as a consensual policy document once none of the members registers a formal disagreement. It also reflects power relations that serve to silence potential opponents to the (normally) prevailing French–German consensus; these power relations assert themselves according to the "law

---

[1] To be precise, the EC has its own President at the table, as well as the President of the Commission plus, if the agenda requires, the High Representative of the Union for Foreign Affairs and Security Policy. As specified in Articles 15, 17 and 18 TEU, these officers are direct or indirect procedural creatures of the EC (by nomination or election or appointment), while the only President who is conspicuously absent from the EC is the President of the European Parliament who is entirely independent of EC control.

of anticipated reaction": nobody will table an initiative that can be expected to be vetoed. This unanimity rule represents the smallest common denominator that national top politicians of member states are able to strike a compromise on. If it were otherwise and some kind of qualified majority rule were to apply, the national constituency of presidents or prime ministers who find themselves in the minority could (and certainly would) protest that they have been made subject to some kind of "foreign rule," the rule of the majority countries. This arrangement severely limits the potential *effectiveness* of (the non-legislative, but "impulse-giving") governance by the EC. Its democratic *legitimacy* is limited by the fact that members, while certainly being elected into their offices of prime minister etc., are thereby mandated to serve the good of the *country* in which they have been elected, not that of the *European Union*.[2] Members of the EC thus rule over and make decisions binding populations that have not elected them nor can they vote them out of office.[3] In contrast, members of

---

[2] Again, to be precise: The German *Grundgesetz* mandates in its Article 23,1 that the Federal Republic works towards the "development of the European Union." The role this constitutional mandate plays in elections as well as policy making, however, is wide open to interpretation and overall marginal relative to domestic and other national affairs.

[3] Citizens of democratic Portugal, for instance, simply have no way of voting Angela Merkel out of office as she performs as a member of the European Council – although there are strong empirical indications that this is exactly what they would strongly like to be able to do: According to a 2013 survey, no less than 88 percent of Spaniards surveyed and 82 percent of Italians agreed with the proposition that German influence in the EU is "too great." (As reported in *Der Spiegel* no. 1/2014.)

---

the European Parliament are expressly elected to represent the European citizenry in EU legislation.

The weaknesses[4] of this complex institutional arrangement are well known. They can be described as a greatly distorted principal-agent (PA) relationship. An ideal-typical PA relationship in politics – a normatively undemanding model of what happens in a representative democracy – works as follows. The agent (e.g. a member of parliament or a political party) is delegated and authorized by the principal (the constituency) to represent him in making decisions that collectively bind the people into the substantive domain and territory to which they belong. In so far as he is performing this mission, he acts *for* the people. If he fails to satisfy the expectations of his principal and/or to redeem his own promises, he will be sanctioned (punished through losing votes and risking being deprived of his mandate or office) by the principal who holds him accountable. To the extent this sanctioning capacity of the principal applies, rule is also *by* the people. For that mechanism to be operative, the principal needs transparency, provided by media and other participants in the public sphere, enabling him to attribute, with reasonable accuracy, outcomes to agents. If all of these conditions (delegation, domain-specific and territorially specific competencies, transparency, accountability) are in place, we can speak of a well-functioning PA relation.

This model can serve as a measuring rod for diagnosing deficient PA arrangements such as the EU regime. One deficiency applies when the domain of the

---

[4] More precisely: their character as hybrids of intergovernmental and supranational logics.

agent does not coincide with that of the principal, as it does in the case of the EC. For instance, a national electorate elects a government as its agent, the head of which is entitled to make decisions affecting people *outside* the territorial domain of the principal. To the extent that happens, there are "policy-takers" who have neither authorized the agent to represent them nor are entitled to sanction and thereby "de-authorize" him. This type of deficiency applies to the European Council that operates under the unanimity rule. An even more serious deficiency exists if agents are allowed to make decisions, the consequences of which they cannot be held accountable for by anybody. This applies to depoliticized fiduciary institution such as the ECB, the ECJ and, to the extent it "oversees the application of Union law,"[5] the Commission. In these cases, the roles of principals and agents become merged, since the type of authorization on the basis of which agents act is hardly more than some collegial self-authorization. The problem worsens (see below) the more functions of macroeconomic surveillance institutions such as the ECB and the Commission accumulate, which are institutionally entirely immune from the reach of accountability mechanisms, the extreme case being the conditionality regime imposed by the Troika on debtor states. A third type of institutional deficiency is when an agent is perfectly accountable to the population in its domain yet has very limited scope for agency, as is the case with the EP that is not allowed to do what every "normal" legislative body considers its core competence, namely making taxing and spending decisions, passing a budget law, and

---

[5] Article 17, 1 TEU.

---

initiating legislation.[6] A final flaw of principal-agent relations is present if the chain of delegation/representation gets excessively long: political parties are supposed to represent (decide on behalf of) voters, parliaments the parties and their relative strength, governments the parliament, and a Commissioner represents as an agent the member state government which has appointed him or her as his principal; this extended cascade of agencies can make the idea of representation seem rather hollow.

As Fritz Scharpf has stressed in a number of his writings for a long time, it is precisely those EU institutions that have the *greatest* impact on the daily life of people which are the *farthest removed* from democratic accountability: the European Central Bank, the European Court of Justice, and the European Commission. They are completely depoliticized and thus can act in complete independence of whatever citizens, parties, and parliaments prefer or reject. Again, we face a deep divorce between politics and policy: On the one hand, there is often populist mass politics (including

---

[6] Furthermore, the EP suffers from the anomaly that it does not meet (and will hardly ever obtain) the standard of a "peoples chamber," or a normal legislature; for that, it would have to comply with the "one man one vote" rule and the principle of equal *weight* of each vote. As, for instance, the populations of Germany and Luxemburg relate to each other in quantitative terms as 204:1, the constituency of Luxemburg (or Malta or one day Iceland) would hardly ever agree to be massively downgraded in its representational weight in the EP through an abolition of the rule of "degressive proportionality" currently in force; yet that rule has already been declared "undemocratic" in lower houses by the German Constitutional Court. Cf. Bundesverfassungsgericht 2009, Tz. 274–95.

identity-related "culture wars") that has no perceptible implication for policy making on citizens' core interests and bread-and-butter issues. On the other, there is elitist policy making that has no roots in, no links to, nor legitimation through politics. The promises and appeals by which political power is *acquired* (i.e., *politics*) are disjointed, under the dictate of financial markets, from the purposes of the achievement of which power resources mandated to governments are *effectively employed* and used for the making of *policies*.

Let us now see what happens under conditions of fiscal and monetary crisis, that is, when EU politics shifts into the "emergency register"[7] and great and imminent dangers are on everybody's mind. First of all, emergencies call for *rapid* action – time is short and may not be wasted through deliberation and the time-consuming process and accommodation of conflict. Crisis-induced time pressure "makes a virtue of haste and delegitimizes dissent"; "the stakes are too high to be left to the vagaries of public opinion."[8] Secondly, following formalistically established rules and procedures and thus allowing rapid crisis responses to be delayed would be utterly unwise, as "exceptional measures are called for in exceptional times."[9] If "survival" can be claimed to be at stake, whatever is being done to secure it does not require justification; the only justification is a successful outcome. Times of emergency are times when "the rule book is laid aside." The action that must be taken is to be left to the initiative of experts and removed from the arena of political contestation. The urgency of the situation creates unquestionable necessities which may trump

---

[7] White 2013: 1.
[8] Ibid., 2, 5.
[9] Barroso, as quoted in White 2013: 1.

statutory and even constitutional norms, such as legal objections the ECJ or the German Constitutional Court may eventually come up with concerning the ECB's OMT program. Norms and subsequent judicial objections, to the extent they can be claimed to hinder a rapid and effective response to the emergency, are circumvented and replaced by *ad hoc* decisions and the "hurried creation of new institutions"[10] with a limitless mandate to do "whatever it takes" to prevent disasters. Action must be guided not by what is consented and legally prescribed but by what is "necessary" and to which "there is no alternative." Time pressure, the substitution of decisions for rules and the replacement of accountable politicians with technocratic experts all converge on a radical disempowerment of the principal, the citizenry. A discourse dominates in which looming disasters, emergency, exceptional situations, and existential threats are amalgamated with the irrefutable necessity to rescue and to restore stability and security on the basis of an elaborate "surveillance framework" – a framework designed to detect all kinds of "imbalances" in the financial practices of member states.[11] Instead of integration through law and its obligatory power, we get modes of cooperation that result from direct material coercion and conditionalist blackmail: any refusal to adopt austerity measures and other "reforms" will be punished by the refusal of assistance on which recipients existentially depend. Note that this mode of rule amounts to a direct translation

---

[10] Ibid., 3.

[11] As to its discretionary methods and policy implications, this discourse, including its stress on permanent and comprehensive surveillance, can be seen as a civilian-economic analogue to the "securitization" discourse triggered by the events of 9/11; the common denominator is the emancipation of policy from legal constraints in the name of existential dangers.

of pressure coming from financial markets into pressure the EU exercises against its legally defenseless members. At its worst, the EU functions as a political amplifier of the silent forces of economic power.

However, there is a set of arguments in defense of European integration, namely "conservative" ones, although they originate from the political Left. In a nutshell, proponents of these arguments see European integration that has been accomplished so far as being a process of predominantly "negative" integration in which national borders and their protective functions are demolished for the sake of uninhibited market freedom and border-crossing competition on an (allegedly) "level" playing field. The liberalization of trade, investment, and factor mobility, however, undercuts the capacity of national states to regulate, protect, and intervene in social and political affairs according to democratically established standards of rights and legal regulation. As a consequence, and in spite of largely nominal and fictive reservations of "subsidiarity" granted by the Treaties to member states, the balance that national democratic states have built over decades between the market and the state has been seriously tilted in favor of the former, thus gradually incapacitating democratic politics of justice and social integration, a process that has accelerated under the impact of the debt crisis. Investors and employers who were, to an extent, under the control of national regimes of production and distribution are now, under the regime of pure market freedom and "negative" integration, allowed to escape from its control through all kinds of "exit" options: If they dislike the rules and conditions that are legally valid in one place, they can practice "regime shopping" and relocate, buy, or seek employment elsewhere. Yet it is not only investors and suppliers of goods, labor, and services who are brought into more extended scope of competition with each other; the same applies to states themselves, who are now exposed to the constant pressure to favor, through their policies and tax regimes, capital (after all, the strategic source of their tax base) and economize on the costs of labor and social expenditures so as to prevent investors from turning to exit. States themselves turn into competitors, with other states trying to attract and maintain investment as their basis of tax revenues (as well as employment as their basis of "social peace"). Seen in this light, Europe, through its "negative" mode of integration consisting in the demolition of borders, "barriers to trade," and modes of distribution and social protection within member states that markets judge "inefficient," is a machinery of market liberalization that disempowers states and their democratic constituencies concerning their capacity to make policies that would constrain market forces rather than unleashing them.

Yet this is not the inevitable end of the story. Constitutional theorists Fossum and Menéndez state the problem succinctly: The constitutional structure of the EU "has fostered a huge structural democratic deficit, leading to the disempowering of politics…The constitutionalization of economic freedoms has subjected all national laws to a potential review of European constitutionality, disempowering national political processes to undertake socioeconomic policies that even marginally limit economic freedoms…The national *Sozialer Rechtsstaat* is under suspicion when not in retreat. That would not be dramatic, were it not for the fact that this has not gone hand-in-hand with the restoration of political capabilities at the supranational level."[12] In other words, European integration can conceivably also be of a "positive" sort, compensating for market-inflicted losses of national

---

[12] Fossum and Menéndez 2011: 224 (emphasis omitted).

sovereignty at the supranational level and rebuilding market-constraining political capacities that have been eroded at the level of member states, thereby conserving and restoring a distorted balance at a higher and more inclusive level. For that to happen, however, the EU would have to be turned into a supranational *democracy*,[13] complete with mechanisms of territorial and functional representation, elected legislative bodies, and accountable supranational governing agencies.[14] While there cannot be any doubt that, so far, processes of "negative" integration have consistently outpaced, in fact obstructed, the dynamics of "positive" integration (largely eradicating in the process the political forces standing for the latter), it seems far too early to denounce the EU categorically as *nothing but* a market-making machinery that unequivocally deprives nation states and their constituencies of the political resources of effective "voice."[15] After all, and as I have tried to convince readers, the return to the national arena of policy making seems quite unpromising as an alternative, and the so far largely technocratic regime in place at the EU level is manifestly (if inconsequentially) aware of being in desperate need of at least a semblance of democratic legitimacy.

---

[13] The authors admit that "At this stage, a democratic refounding of the Union is unlikely, bar a sudden and drastic politicization of the European Union which is at the same time sufficiently focused so as to bear constitutional fruit." (Ibid.)
[14] A rich variety of constitutional theories and proposals by which this could be accomplished has been developed throughout the crisis experience and even before. Schmitter 2000; Habermas 2012; Franzius and Preuss 2012; Guérot and Leonard 2011; Spinelli Group 2013; Tsoukalis 2014. The discussion of these constitutional proposals remains largely outside of the concerns of the present book.
[15] Hirschman 1970.

10

Redistribution Across State Borders and Social Divides

As we have seen, the EU in general and the Euro zone in particular are divided by pervasive and multiple conflicts. North *vs* south, old *vs* new member states, renationalization *vs* deeper integration, protest politics *vs* technocratic policy making, supranationalism *vs* intergovernmentalism, core *vs* periphery, neoliberalism *vs* a Leftist vision of re-embedding democratic capitalism are crisscrossing political and ideological cleavages which do not add up to a consistent pattern. Rather than leading to the formation of a clear-cut "ruling ideology" *vs* a mobilized opposition with an agenda of its own, a fuzzy pattern of multiple and cross-cutting conflicts paralyzes agency and renders the social dynamics involved sterile. Competing frames and definitions of the situation create confusion and disorientation, while at least for some participants in the Euro zone, those most exposed to the economic labor market and social crisis in the periphery, the situation gets ever more unbearable in terms of their income, security, and access to services. For others in the core member states, the crisis is a remote disturbance of the normal ups and downs of economic events that governments will do their best to prevent from spilling over so as to affect "us."

I am not sure whether one should share the modest hopes of those who expect that a strong electoral showing of the populist anti-European Right in the EP will catalyze in response a strong strategic initiative of left and center European parties. Nor can I see a significant political impact and mobilizational resonance among those who advocate innovative designs for the building of democratic institutions at the European level. The blatant "democratic deficit" and the resulting weakness of EU-wide policy capacity seems to be a disorder that mostly intellectual elites take issue with, while it does not cause much pain to others. The democratization of the EU's decision making simply does not seem to have much of a "mass base" as a demand, in contrast to highly popular complaints about the overly stringent ruling and bureaucratic interference of the Commission into "our" affairs. If the project of renovating and democratizing the institutional *forms* of the EU and the Euro zone is not something that, by itself, can stir up the passions and ambitions of broad constituencies, then perhaps the *substantive* issues of social justice and of the corresponding policies and policy capacities have a greater potential for the mobilization of a kind of agency capable of carrying out viable responses to the crisis.

It is this latter perspective I want to explore in this final chapter. Probably needless to say, the distinction of form and content of policy making is at best a temporal one; once the "right" issues are on the table, the issue will follow of how (through which hitherto unavailable institutionalized competencies and procedures) to deal

with them.[1] So, what are the "right" issues that have
the potential for politicizing the EU? In my view, any
valid answer to this question must pass a triple test: It
must be an issue that already is adopted by the EU as
one of its responsibilities and promises; it must have the
potential to mobilize political agency; and it must, once
it is moved up the agenda of policy, hold a promise of
helping to address the economic crisis effectively. The
issue of *improving social justice through social security
and income redistribution across member states and
social classes* is (arguably the only) one that clearly satisfies all three of these criteria: it redeems the ambition of
the EU having a "social dimension" (as specified in Art.
3,3 TEU and Art. 151 TFEU); it corresponds to the
manifest interests of the growing proportion of EU-
Europeans threatened by poverty and precariousness[2]
who can rightly and powerfully claim that it is by now
their turn to be "bailed out"; and it promises to contribute through the expansionary effects of enhanced
effective demand to the boosting of employment and
fiscal revenues. The moment that these kinds of redistributive policies were widely seen to figure credibly and
consistently on the EU's agenda, reasons to worry about
a lack of broad interest in and mass engagement with
matters of European policies are likely to evaporate
instantaneously.

Let us take a closer look at the extreme case in its
overall configuration (if not so in view of some of its
component indicators). A country in which the GDP
shrank by 23.5 percent in the course of five years and
investment by 58.4 percent, where unemployment is at

---

[1] As modern theorists of architecture know well: "Form
follows function!"
[2] Standing 2011.

26.7 percent of the work force and the rate of youth unemployment at 60.4 percent, where 2.3 million (of a total of 2.8 million) households have tax debts they cannot service, where pensions are the main source of income for 48.6 percent of families and where 3.5 million employed people have to support 4.7 million unemployed or inactive people – such a country, as Wolfgang Münchau[3] rightly observes the Greek condition of Spring 2014, "is not in recession. Nor is it recovering. It has collapsed."

There is no shortage of policy proposals, which serve as proof that there *are* "alternatives." A rather sizeable write-down of sovereign debt ("restructuration") is needed to reduce the remaining debt to sustainable levels; the need to recapitalize "systemic" banks that suffer losses as a consequence is to be taken care of by the ECB, which may also rely on Cyprus-style "bail-ins." EU-wide tax harmonization applying to direct taxes would help to disincentivize "regime shopping" practices and transnational capital flight. Budget deficits can be addressed not just by austerity measures and "internal" devaluation; they can also be solved by increasing taxes on high income and wealth, even by forcing the wealthy to buy government bonds. Indirect taxes have the great advantage that their tax base cannot flee the country and the well-known downside that their incidence is regressive: the relatively poor spend greater parts of their income and thus shoulder a greater proportion of the burden of indirect taxes. Why not apply a progressive schedule on consumption (income minus investment/savings per tax year); the progressive taxation of individual consumption thus measured would replace the flat sales tax, thus combining the

---

[3] Münchau 2014.

advantages, in terms of distributional fairness,[4] of direct and indirect taxation? Furthermore, proposals have been made to Europeanize the systems of unemployment insurance[5] and social assistance/poverty relief,[6] the realization of which would certainly boost, as a side effect, the mass identification with Europe as a political entity capable of alleviating problems of distributional justice. Moreover, without violating the "subsidiarity" principle enshrined in the Treaties, a European legislation could be launched that specifies maximum permissible Gini-coefficients (perfectly in line with the EU's stated goal of reaching "cohesion") for member state societies, with the level inversely tied to their current GDP per capita values. *How* member states meet their Gini targets that correspond to their GDP performance (through taxation, through poverty relief, through minimum wages, through basic income schemes) remains entirely a matter of national legislation and would thus conform to the "subsidiarity" requirements of the Treaties. Also, commercial banks could be prohibited to accept deposits from financial investors who can be identified as fleeing their debt-troubled countries. Carefully targeted and time-limited constraints on capital mobility cannot seriously be considered sacrilegious, and parties advocating such measures may well gain at the polls as a consequence.

The NEET problem (young people aged 15 to 24 years who are "not in employment, education or training," thus deprived of any institutional shelter that is available for this age category)[7] has begun to be

---

[4] I am referring here to current PhD research of Max Held.
[5] Dullien 2008.
[6] van Parijs 2013.
[7] Cf. Eurofound 2012.

recognized by the Commission as a virtual time bomb. It has resulted in a Council recommendation to member states to introduce a "Youth Guarantee" providing for some kind of such shelter within four months of the incidence of an individual's NEET condition. An ILO report[8] undertook a cost-benefit analysis of the program and found that Youth Guarantee schemes introduced in the entire Euro zone would cost 21 bn Euros pa, or 0.22 percent of Euro zone GDP. Compared with that amount, total costs (in terms of transfers, lost income, and lost tax revenues) of *failing* to adopt the program were estimated by a Eurofound study to amount to 153 bn Euros (1.21 percent of GDP). That calculation suggests that Youth Guarantee is a fantastically profitable business proposal, with its return on capital (gains plus losses avoided) of more than 700 percent pa. But as this gain does not constitute a property right of anyone (but rather would benefit "all of us") this investment is at best reluctantly implemented, while NEET rates mount everywhere in the EU with the exception of Luxemburg, Austria, Sweden, and Germany[9] – a compelling illustration of the damages austerity inflicts.

These and other policy proposals can largely be implemented through European legislation, particularly if macroeconomic stabilization problems combine with political conflicts to push the constraints of European social policy making outwards. The problem is that before that can happen, a basic "mental reframing" of the situation is called for in that the prevailing "methodological nationalism" code of "nation *vs* nation" must be partly substituted and supplemented by a code

---

[8] ILO 2012.
[9] European Trade Union Institute 2013: 77.

of "losers *vs* winners" of the crisis, if not socioeconomic "class *vs* class" or "generation *vs* generation."

The invigoration of anything resembling "Social Europe" can proceed by two types of fiscal measures (and any combination thereof): Trivially, it can operate on the revenue side of budgets and on the expenditure side. The former may include measures known as "hair cuts," "bail-ins," Tobin taxes on financial transactions, one-time taxes on big properties and various forms of debt-mutualization and risk-pooling in social security systems, for instance a partial Europeanization of unemployment insurance,[10] a redistributive measure that would imply effects both across member states' borders and social divides within them; it would also serve as an automatic stabilizer of effective demand. Here, it would also help to achieve a harmonization of (corporate) income tax throughout the EU as it would limit the scope of "regime shopping" for tax evasion. The other type of fiscal measures involves the standardization of minimum levels of social expenditures, be it for the social budget as a whole or be it for specific policy areas such as pensions, poverty relief, etc. For instance, given the unrestricted Euro-mobility that became fully effective in January 2014 and the ensuing conflicts and local problems of poverty-driven migration from Romania and Bulgaria, migrant-receiving member states will push for a better policy of poverty relief and child benefits in countries of emigration so as to diminish poverty and its migration effects.

There can be little doubt that the leadership of the Commission and other top European institutions has quite clearly perceived the urgency of undertaking

---

[10] This proposal has been advanced and elaborated in numerous publications and policy papers by Sebastian Dullien.

credible efforts toward a "Strengthening [of] the Social Dimension of the Economic and Monetary Union."[11] A coordinated system of minimum wages would help to combat practices of "social dumping." Van Parijs (2013) has proposed the adoption of a "Euro-dividend" as a modest income floor of 200 Euros per month per person to which every legal EU resident would be entitled, regardless of age, labor market, or family status. This could be financed out of the combined revenue of VAT, Tobin tax and carbon tax and provide a "firm floor on which one can rely in all circumstances," which in turn would facilitate mobility in space and flexibility in working time, all of which appears highly desirable from a functional point of view. As to the motivational effects of such a scheme: "It would give everyone a tangible share in part of the overall material gain that can be safely attributed to the very existence of the EU... The prosperity would then be clearly seen to benefit each of its parts – member states, regions, and households," an effect which would establish a strong link between citizens' individual material interests and the EU. Note that these and similar proposals share two features. First, a claim to tax-financed transfers is tied to recipients' identity as *citizens*, not that of being a market participant/employee or a person in need. Second, the norm of justice on which such policies of redistribution are based is not egalitarianism but republicanism and what has been called "the doctrine of sufficiency."[12]

There are, however, two major institutional obstacles hindering significant progress in redeeming EU-wide social policy ambitions. One resides in the fact that EP

---

[11] European Commission 2013.
[12] The classical source is Frankfurt 1987.

and Council do not have the fiscal rights that ordinary legislative bodies have: they can neither tax nor generate revenues through the issuing of bonds, although there is some leeway for issuing "project bonds."[13] The EU budget is decided on by a unanimous vote of the member states. The budget is limited to ca one percent of the EU's GDP, of which a major portion of more than one third is earmarked for agricultural subsidies. In a word, the EU so far does not control the resources necessary in order to gain a significant redistributive role of its own. The other institutional obstacle has to do with the fact that most social policy making, as far as involves monetary transfers, is strictly reserved for decisions within the national arenas of member states – the so-called "subsidiarity" principle of the Roman Catholic social doctrine, laid down in article 153,4 TFEU. Given these two severe constraints, the social policy role of the EU is largely restricted to methods such as sponsoring Social Dialogue, conducting the Open Method of Coordination, monitoring national employment and social policies and their achievements, and defining social policy goals to be implemented by member states through the overall Europe 2020 strategy.

László Andor (2013a, b), EU-Commissioner for Employment, Social Affairs, and Inclusion, calls for the restoration of the social dimension of the EMU consisting in "rules, procedures and capacities at European level that can sustain the potential for real convergence." The aspiration is to "reconcile economic efficiency and social equity in EMU-level decision making." For that, clearly more is needed than the conventional toolbox of monitoring indicators, issuing recommendations and

---

[13] Cf., for instance, http://www.cliffordchance.com/briefings/2013/09/europe_2020_projectbondsanewfinancin.html.

appeals to national and supra-national social partners and their social dialogues. What is needed, according to Commissioner Andor, is an EMU-level fiscal capacity that would allow for supporting recovery from cyclical downturns in target countries, an EMU-level unemployment benefit scheme, and binding employment and social standards through EU legislation.

While it is true that (re)distributive measures require mechanisms of *input* legitimacy at the supra-national level, it is also the case that policy *outputs* aiming at objectives of greater social security and more expenditures for education and health may well by themselves *generate* legitimacy for the EU, which it can bolster by enhancing and making more credible its "social dimension." "Positive" integration and "input" legitimacy can well be seen as being related in a loop of circular causation. Thus those two major constraints are themselves a matter of dispute and contestation; they are likely to become more so and eventually begin to crumble as the ongoing divergence of social and economic fates between the core and the periphery deepens.[14] The Commission's perceived need to gain control over issues of "macroeconomic stabilization" leads it to think aloud about providing "an insurance system to pool the risks of economic shocks across Member States." It also intimates that "such measures would require a substantial Treaty change," a "fundamental overhaul of the Treaties"[15] as dictated by

---

[14] This is evidently a slow process. All the more should EU officials restrain themselves, as a matter of common decency, when blaming deficit countries for "reform fatigue," an ailment that has afflicted the EU authorities to a similar if less excusable extent.

[15] European Commission 2013: 10–11.

mounting problems of macroeconomic governance. Strict adherence to "subsidiarity" would make that governance even less effective than it has been in the past. Moreover, moves to strengthen the scope of EP and Council to engage in policies of redistribution will not only be driven by the functional requirement to strengthen effective demand through "automatic stabilizers," but equally by the perceived need to reconcile the protest and populist mobilization of those who have grown too numerous, and their voices too loud, to be ignored any longer. Nothing less will do than a carefully designed set of EU-sponsored material entitlements, this time not destined to the rescue of banks and states but to those workers, unemployed, youths, pensioners, and citizens who are most severely affected by the financial crisis.

References

Agamben, Giorgio (2013) The endless crisis as an instrument of power: In conversation with Giorgio Agamben. Verso Books, http://www.versobooks.com/blogs/1318-the-endless-crisis-as-an-instrument-of-power-in-conversation-with-giorgio-agamben

Anderson, Perry (2009) *The New Old World*. Verso Books, London.

Andor, László (2013a) Developing the social dimension of a deep and genuine economic and monetary union. European Policy Centre, Policy Brief, http://ec.europa.eu/commission_2010-2014/andor/documents/developing_social_dimensio-en.pdf

—— (2013b) Strengthening the European social model. Speech given at conference "Progressive paths to growth and social cohesion. A future agenda for Eastern and Central Europe" on November 11, 2013, Vilnius, http://europa.eu/rapid/press-release_SPEECH-13-901_en.htm?locale=en

Armingeon, Klaus and Guthmann, Kai (2013) Democracy in crisis? The declining support for national democracy in European countries, 2007–2011. *European Journal of Political Research*, 20 December 2013, doi: 10.1111/1475-6765.12046.

Bank of International Settlements (2014) BIS Quarterly Review, March 2014, http://www.bis.org/publ/qtrpdf/r_qt1403.pdf

References

Barker, Alex (2013) "EU ministers set to define banking union." *Financial Times*, December 17.

Bechtel, Michael, Hainmueller, Jens, and Yotam Margalit (2014) Preferences for international redistribution: The divide over the eurozone bailouts. *American Journal of Political Science*, forthcoming.

Bertelsmann-Stiftung (2012) Wirtschaftliche Folgen eines Euro-Austritts der südeuropäischen Mitgliedsstaaten. Policy Brief 2012/06, http://www.bertelsmann-stiftung.de/cps/rde/xbcr/SID-4837FF17-837E03F3/bst/xcms_bst_dms_36638_36639_2.pdf

Blanchard, Olivier and Daniel Leigh (2013) Growth forecast errors and fiscal multipliers. IMF Working Paper, WP/13/1, International Monetary Fund.

Bofinger, Peter, Habermas, Jürgen, and Julia Nida-Rümelin (2012) "Einspruch gegen die Fassadendemokratie." Frankfurter Allgemeine Zeitung, August 3.

Bolaffi, Angelo (2013) *Cuore Tedesco. Il modello Germania.* Rome: Donzelli.

Bundesverfassungsgericht (2009) Judgment of the German Constitutional Court on the Treaty of Lisbon, 2 BvE 2/08, June 30, 2009, http://www.bverfg.de/entscheidungen/es20090630_2bve000208.html

Crouch, Colin (2004) *Post-Democracy*. Polity, Cambridge.

Deutschmann, Christoph (2011) Limits to financialization. Sociological analyses of the financial crisis. In *Archives Européennes de Sociologie*, 52, 3 (2011), 347–89.

Dullien, Sebastien (2008) Eine Arbeitslosenversicherung für die Euro-Zone. Stiftung Wissenschaft und Politik, SWP-Studien 2008/ S 01, http://www.swp-berlin.org/de/publikationen/swp-studien-de/swp-studien-detail/article/arbeitslosenversicherung_fuer_die_eurozone.html

Enderlein, Henrik (2013a) Solidarität in der Europäischen Union – Die ökonomische Perspektive. In Calliess, Christian (ed.) *Europäische Solidarität und Nationale Identität: Überlegungen im Kontext der Krise des Euroraum.* Mohr Siebeck, Tübingen, 83–97.

—— (2013b) Das erste Opfer der Krise ist die Demokratie: Wirtschaftspolitik und ihre Legitimation in der Finanzmarktkrise 2008–2013. *Politische Vierteljahresschrift*, 54 (4), 714–39.

References

European Commission (2013) Communication from the Commission to the European Parliament and the Council. Strengthening the social dimension of the economic and monetary union. COM(2013) 690, October 2, Brussels.

Eurofound (2012) NEETs – Young people not in employment, education or training: Characteristics, costs and policy responses in Europe. Publications Office of the European Union, Luxemburg.

European Trade Union Institute (2013) Benchmarking Working Europe 2013. ETUI, Brussels.

Flassbeck, Heiner (2012) *Zehn Mythen der Krise*. Suhrkamp, Berlin.

Fossum, John Erik and Menéndez, Agustín José (2011) *The Constitution's Gift: A Constitutional Theory for a Democratic European Union*. Rowman & Littlefield Publishers, Plymouth.

Frankfurt, Harry (1987) Equality as a moral ideal. *Ethics*, 98 (1), 21–43.

Franzius, Claudio and Ulrich K. Preuß (2012) *Die Zukunft der Europäischen Demokratie*. Schriften zu Europa Band 7, Heinrich Böll Stiftung, Berlin.

Giles, Chris and Kate Allen (2013) "Southeastern shift: The new leaders of global economic growth." *Financial Times*, June 4, http://www.ft.com/intl/cms/s/0/b0bd38b0-ccfc-11e2-9efe-00144feab7de.html#axzz2z3FZtpHO

Gammelin, Cerstin and Raimund Löw (2014) *Europa's Strippenzieher*. Econ, Berlin.

Gordon, Robert J. (2012) Is US Economic growth over? Faltering Innovation confronts the six headwinds. The National Bureau of Economic Research, NBER Working Paper No. 18315, August.

Gordon, Sarah (2014) "Give them some credit." *Financial Times*, February 19, http://www.ft.com/intl/cms/s/0/3d260 e6c-956b-11e3-8371-00144feab7de.html#axzz2z3FZtp HO

Guérot, Ulrike and Mark Leonard (2011) The New German question: How Europe can get the Germany it needs. European Council on Foreign Relations, April (30).

Haas, Ernst B. (1961) International integration: The European and the universal process. *International Organization*, 15 (3), 366–92.

References

Habermas, Jürgen (2012) *The Crisis of the European Union*. Polity, Cambridge.
—— (2013a) Demokratie oder Kapitalismus? *Blätter für deutsche und international Politik*, 2013 (5), 59–70.
—— (2013b) *Im Sog der Technokratie*. Suhrkamp, Berlin
Hirschman, Albert O. (1970) *Exit, Voice and Loyalty: Responses to Decline in Firms, Organizations, and States*. Harvard University Press, Harvard.
—— (1977) *The Passions and the Interests: Political Arguments For Capitalism Before Its Triumph*. Princeton University Press, Princeton, NJ.
Holmes, Stephen and Cass R. Sunstein (1999) *The Cost of Rights: Why Liberty Depends on Taxes*. W. W. Norton & Company, New York.
International Labour Organization (2012) Eurozone job crisis: Trends and policy responses. International Institute for Labour Studies, Geneva.
—— (2014) Global Employment Trends 2014. International Labour Office, Geneva.
Issing, Otmar (2014) "Get your finances in order and stop blaming Germany." *Financial Times*, March 25, http://www.ft.com/intl/cms/s/0/9a1636a6-b2c1-11e3-8038-00144feabdc0.html#axzz2z3FZtpHO
Leonard, Mark and José Ignacio Torreblanca (2013) "The remarkable rise of continental Euroscepticism." *Guardian*, April 24, http://www.theguardian.com/commentisfree/2013/apr/24/continental-euroscepticism-rise
Mair, Peter (2007) Political opposition and the European union. *Government and Opposition*, 42 (1), 1–17.
Mak, Geert (2012) *Was, wenn Europa scheitert?* München: Patheon.
Marsh, David (2013) *Europe's Deadlock: How the Euro Crisis Could Be Solved – and Why It Won't Happen*. Yale University Press, New Haven.
Mundell, Robert A. (1961) A theory of optimum currency areas. *The American Economic Review* 51 (4), 657–65.
Münchau, Wolfgang (2014) "This could be the moment for Greece to default." *Financial Times*, April 13, http://www.ft.com/intl/cms/s/0/26f7a326-c0d6-11e3-bd6b-00144feabdc0.html#axzz30G1bSfk9
O'Connor, James (1979) *The Fiscal Crisis of the State*. Saint Martin's Press, New York.

References

Offe, Claus (1976) Crisis of crisis management: Elements of a political crisis theory. *International Journal of Politics*, 6 (3), 29–67.

—— (2006) Is there, or can there be, a "European society"? In Keane, John (ed.) *Civil Society. Berlin Perspectives*, Berghahn Books, New York: 169–88.

—— (2013) Shared social responsibility – A concept in search of its political meaning and promise. In *Shared Social Responsibility. Putting Theory into Practice*. Strasburg: Council of Europe Publishing: 29–47.

Peel, Quentin (2012) "Germany: A lonely path." *Financial Times*, June 6, http://www.ft.com/intl/cms/s/533541e8-afce-11e1-a025-00144feabdc0.html

Platzer, Hans-Wolfgang (2014) Rolling back or expanding European integration? *Friedrich Ebert Stiftung*, February 2014, http://library.fes.de/pdf-files/id/ipa/10527.pdf

Polanyi, K. (2001[1944]) *The Great Transformation: The Political and Economic Origins of Our Time*. Beacon Press, Boston.

Posner, Richard A. (2010) *The Crisis of Capitalist Democracy*. Harvard University Press, Cambridge.

Rachman, Gideon (2014) "Courts, voters and the threat of another Euro crisis." *Financial Times*, February 10, http://www.ft.com/intl/cms/s/0/ad524ca8-9031-11e3-a776-00144feab7de.html

Reinhart, Carmen M., and Kenneth S. Rogoff (2009) *This Time Is Different: Eight Centuries of Financial Folly*, Princeton University Press, Princeton.

Rodrik, Dani (2011) *The Globalization Paradox: Democracy and the Future of the World Economy*. W.W. Norton & Company, New York and London.

—— (2013) Europe's way out. Project Syndicate, June 12, 2013, http://www.project-syndicate.org/commentary/saving-the-long-run-in-the-eurozone-by-dani-rodrik

Scharpf, Fritz W. (2011) Monetary union, fiscal crisis and the preemption of democracy. Max Planck Institute for the Study of Societies, MPifG Discussion Paper 11/11.

—— (2014) The costs of non-disintegration: The case of the European monetary union. In Eppler, Annegret and Henrik Scheller (eds.) *Zur Konzeptionalisierung europäischer Desintegration: Zug und Gegenkräfte im europäischen Integrationsprozess*, Nomos, Baden-Baden, pp. 165–84.

References

Schäfer, Wolf (2013) "Die Eurozone leidet unter intern verzerrten Wechselkursen." *Frankfurter Allgemeine Zeitung*, August 27, http://www.faz.net/aktuell/wirtschaft/gastbeitrag-die-eurozone-leidet-unter-intern-verzerrten-wechselkursen-11868775.html

Schmitter, Philippe C. (2000) *How To Democratize the European Union...And Why Bother?* Rowan & Littlefield Publishers, Lanham.

Schmitz, Gregor Peter and Soros, George (2014) *Wetten auf Europa. Warum Deutschland den Euro retten muss, um sich selbst zu retten.* Deutsche Verlags Anstalt, Stuttgart.

Spinelli Group (2013) *A fundamental law of the European Union.* Bertelsmann, Gütersloh.

Standing, Guy (2011) *The Precariat: The New Dangerous Class.* Bloomsbury Academic, London.

Streeck, Wolfgang (2009) *Re-forming Capitalism: Institutional Change in the German Political Economy.* Oxford University Press, Oxford.

—— (2013) The construction of a moral duty for the Greek people to repay their national debt. *Socio-Economic Review*, 2013 (11): 614–20.

—— (2014) *Buying Time: The Delayed Crisis of Democratic Capitalism.* Verso Books, London.

Thompson, John B. (2012) The metamorphosis of a crisis. In Castells, Manuel, Caraça, João, and Gustavo Cardoso (eds.) *Aftermath. The Cultures of the Economic Crisis*, Oxford University Press, Oxford, pp. 59–81.

Tsoukalis, Loukas (2014) *The Unhappy State of the Union.* Policy Network, London.

van Parijs, Philippe (2013) The Euro-dividend. *Social Europe Journal*, July 3, 2013, http://www.social-europe.eu/2013/07/the-euro-dividend/

White, Jonathan (2013) Emergency Europe. *Political Studies*, 13 September, 2013, doi: 10.1111/1467-9248.12072.

Yardley, Jim (2014) "Spain, land of 10 pm dinners, asks if it's time to reset clock." *New York Times*, February 17, http://www.nytimes.com/2014/02/18/world/europe/spain-land-of-10-pm-dinners-ponders-a-more-standard-time.html

Zürn, Michael and De Wilde, Pieter (2012) Can the politicization of European integration be reversed? *Journal of Common Market Studies*, 50, 137–53.